This book is dedicated to the memory
of my late wife, Jenifer, who gave me
such a wonderful family.
Her wisdom and unselfish support
throughout my career allowed me to achieve
more than I could ever have done on my own.

MEMOIR OF A MEDIUM MAN

for Valerie
as Michael
with best
wishes ad
thanks for
years of
friendship

Paul

Matador
9 Priory Business Park
Wistow Road
Kibworth Beauchamp
Leicestershire LE8 0RX
Telephone: 0116 279 2299
email: books@troubadour.co.uk
web: www.troubadour.co.uk/matador

ISBN 978-1-78901-738-0

British Library Cataloguing in Publication Data
A catalogue record for this book is available from the British Library

Printed and bound by CPI Group (UK) Ltd, Croydon, CR0 4YY
Design, typesetting and production by John Haycock

Twin Zebras Productions
5 Strand on the Green
London W4 3PQ
Telephone: 020 8987 8742

MEMOIR OF A MEDIUM MAN

BY
PAUL BONNER
WITH CECILIA COLESHAW

Acknowledgements and thanks

Cecilia Coleshaw started as a very helpful PA. However her role grew to include research and editorial wisdom. At that point it became apparent that she had become a valuable contributing author, for which she gets a credit.

Pamela Dear knows more about the birth and development of Channel Four than anyone else. She has been a particularly valuable point of reference in relation to press coverage of the channel.

Rosie Gleeson is the Information and Archives Manager, Channel Four Television and has connections with the BBC and other television archivists which have proved invaluable in writing this book.

Eddie Mirzoeff is someone who features in the book as a colleague but he has remained a friend since we first worked together in the 1960s. His continuing dialogue has benefited me – and therefore also this *Memoir*.

Sir Jeremy Isaacs was introduced to me by Eddie Mirzoeff in the sixties. Little did I think then that Jeremy and I would become partners in the great adventure of setting up a complete new television channel – Channel Four. We remain friends and he is another who has contributed to my vision of public service broadcasting and its purpose.

Alison Bonner produced a detailed *curriculum vitae* as a speech for my 80th birthday dinner. It was to become the original seed for this memoir. She made my life sound interesting!

Neil Bonner and **Mark Bonner**, my two sons, now high achievers in their own right, who in their teenage years became the brothers I never had.

John Haycock took on the design, typesetting and production of this book and bore with patience the many last-minute changes that were required

To all others who have contributed valuable facts and memories in conversation during the writing of this book and are un-credited here, please accept my gratitude.

Contents

Combat Stress and this book

I first came to know of Combat Stress and its work during my national service when it was still known by its foundation title, The Ex-Servicemen's Mental Welfare Society. Fortunately the medic treating two of my men who had been ambushed by the Muslim Brotherhood in the Suez Canal Zone in 1953 knew about the organisation's work.

The charity was founded in 1919 to help mentally damaged servicemen returning from the First World War. In those days what we call Post Traumatic Stress Disorder (PTSD) was known as 'shell shock'. Its sufferers were not well treated – largely through ignorance. Many found it impossible to settle back into civilian life without help.

Nowadays the charity provides counselling and trauma-focused therapy as well as occupational therapy. Combat Stress now has centres in different regions to provide treatment for servicemen returning from active service with PTSD.

£2 from the sale of each copy of this book will go to Combat Stress but if people wish to donate more they can pay directly to the charity.

If you would like to donate to Combat Stress (Charity Registration No. 206002, SC038828 in Scotland) please visit combatstress.org.uk/donate, call the team on 01372 587151 or write to Tyrwhitt House, Oaklawn Road, Leatherhead KT22 0BX.

Foreword

In 1955 BBC Television was still a young medium and I was still a young man. The independence of the BBC was guaranteed by Royal Charter and the purpose of broadcasting in that Charter was to "inform, educate and entertain." In the early days, when transmission was mostly 'live', part of the entertainment was when things went wrong on screen, a factor that the audience enjoyed.

The early period of post-war BBC television offered opportunities for this new visual medium. There is always a nostalgia for the good times of an early career, but we were amongst the pioneers of a medium still discovering what it could and couldn't do and, importantly, what it could achieve for the audience.

For more than half the population that period has been either forgotten or was never known, so it seems worthwhile to put on record what it was like to work in television, and the good and bad things that I achieved

with it. Another factor was the people. The BBC in particular attracted the brightest and many of the best. The demands of live television – that is pictures and sound transmitted as they happened – were considerable. As a producer or director you needed acute vision, quick reactions and the ability to do, see and hear several things at once. It was a wonderful challenge and I revelled in it.

Working for the BBC at that time was to give me a further benefit which I had failed to achieve because I didn't get into university. At the BBC I got tertiary education 'on the hoof', as it were, working with people of immense experience and many of them with a communicative intellect. Broadcasting has to reach a wide audience and some of the foremost minds of the period were attracted to work at or appear on the BBC. It was a real privilege to work with such people at such a time.

CHAPTER ONE

A thrust too far?

There was a nasty metallic grinding sound, the stench of burning oil and we fell out of the sky like a stone. The helicopter spun round and round in the sand like a mad beetle. The door that had been on my left was now above me. I flung it open and looked back. There were flames building. "I think we'd better get out fast," I shouted to my cameraman and Steve, the pilot. Steve's response was "Hang on — I'd better get my log book, there's bound to be an enquiry," while the cameraman was searching for his light meter. Luckily the flames were dying

"There are old helicopter pilots and there are bold helicopter pilots, but as far as I know, there are no old, bold helicopter pilots." Peter Pekowski, pilot

down and we all succeeded in climbing out, shaken, but intact. As we did so there was a roaring sound and in a cloud of dust down the runway came fire engines, ambulances and US Air Force police. As they screeched to a halt beside us, saw we were safe and that the flames had nearly burned out, there were looks of real disappointment on their faces.

It was 1971 and I was filming at Palmdale in the Californian desert, on Lockheed's aerodrome test runway where the first giant jumbo jet engines designed by Rolls-Royce, the RB211s, were being tested on their three-jet jumbo TriStar prototype.

I wanted to use a helicopter to get shots of the TriStar with its engines against the snow of the High Sierras, inland from Los Angeles and, in the way that Americans have, Lockheed was very cooperative with arrangements for filming. Normally we would have filmed from the observer plane that always flew with any prototype, so there would be a record if anything went wrong. But the PR at Lockheed had said "You don't need the Sabre, Mr Bonner. We've got a chopper that we were developing for 'Nam and it will be better for your cameraman. It goes so fast it can loop the loop and will certainly

"We've got a chopper that goes so fast it can loop the loop and will certainly keep up with the TriStar"

keep up with the TriStar." I thought this was a good idea because it would enable us to take a wider range of shots. We finished by filming the bumps and go-arounds: puffs of smoke from the wheels touching the runway and the plane pulling off again and circling round. We got the shots and were preparing to land. We were 30 feet up, moving forward at virtually ten knots over sand beside the runway, and it would have been a safe landing but for one factor – Lockheed had never got round to testing this prototype helicopter for hard landings. The mechanism that allowed the helicopter to go so fast forward without vibration had come away from the centre of the rotor and tipped the machine over on its side.

The helicopter was a mess, but the crew and I got away with little more than a cracked rib and broken thumb between us, thanks to none of us having undone our seat-belts during the flight. To my surprise Daniel Haughton, the chairman

The Rolls-Royce RB211 engine (left) on a VC10 test aircraft – of greater power than the total of the two Avon engines mounted opposite

of Lockheed, came to visit us in hospital. We later learned he was very wary of the media because the American papers were on to a story about Lockheed incentivising Philippine Airlines with a large discount to take the first delivery of the TriStar.

Lockheed's TriStar, with its Rolls-Royce engines, had a competitor, another three-engine jumbo jet from McDonnell Douglas. This rivalry between two similar aircraft of a new type was intense, leading Rolls-Royce to try to make short cuts in the design of the new giant fan turbine that was the RB211. This revolutionary new engine would more than double the thrust of previous jets. It was rumoured that to test the new titanium turbine blades, frozen chickens were fired at them from close range. It was this competition and its financial demands that brought down the giant of British engineering.

During our research we discovered that Rolls-Royce engineering had a relationship with the Manchester Business School, whereby their junior accountancy staff would go to the school to further their financial education. They were asked to take with them the company's accounts for the year. When the Canadian Professor Carson, who handled these students, looked at Rolls-Royce's accounts he noticed that major aspects of research for the jumbo RB211 were accounted on the asset side rather than the debit side. There was a reason for this. At that period, the early 1970s, the board-appointed managing director of the Aero Engine division was almost always taken from the senior engineering executives. They were great engineers, but their knowledge of accountancy was minimal. To David Huddie, the post-holder in 1971, the research into which money had been poured was an asset – even though it was actually, in the case of the development of the RB211, a massive expenditure. Because government money was involved in the development of the project, this fatal flaw, which led to the querying of the accounts by the auditors, was given a wider audience. Ultimately the then Labour Minister for Industry, Tony Wedgwood Benn, saw the only route out of the difficulty was nationalisation. So Rolls-Royce Bankrupt became Rolls-Royce 1971, a nationalised industry under the direction of Dr Beeching – the man who had cut all non-profitable rail lines when the nationalised British Rail was created.

In 'Dragon', my first dinghy

As with much television research, a great deal was owed to chance. While I was overseeing the negotiations between BBC Lighting staff and Rolls-Royce electricians in the PR office I saw my writer, the journalist John Pearson, look suddenly very happy, if rather flushed. Afterwards I asked him what had caused him such pleasure. "I was talking to Irene, the lady who runs the PR office, and asked her 'where were you when the company went bust?' She replied 'I was in bed with the finance director, while the world's press was ringing us to ask for quotes'!" This was that rare event in television: direct access to the inside story.

Decades later, because I had made a film on Rolls-Royce, I was invited – by Lockheed, in fact – to fly on the show TriStar with my family. Fellow passengers included VIPs such as Michael Heseltine, of Westland crisis fame, then the Minister for Aerospace, who had also brought his children. While he and I were talking about the prospects of success for the TriStar, our teenage sons were raiding the hospitality drinks trolley and rolling about the plane in a state of alcoholic delight. Michael Heseltine and I looked at one another. He shrugged and so did I.

Flying was something that I had been attracted to at a very early age. I would have liked to have learned to fly in later life, but I didn't have the money to take lessons and the RAF failed me on the grounds of poor eyesight. When we moved to Leigh-on-Sea at the end of the war, having my own boat became my substitute pleasure and excitement.

Ironically, my enthusiasm for things aeronautical led me, at the age of 12, to write to Rolls-Royce, asking them to explain how a jet engine worked. This was a new form of propulsion developed at the end of the war, which had been kept fairly secret. Rolls-Royce very kindly sent me explanatory diagrams of the apparent magic of air going in the front and flames heating it up to a point where it was powerful enough to push an aeroplane along, thereby replacing propellers in a way that was to change the world.

CHAPTER TWO

To school with a gas mask

That helicopter crash was the eighth of nine brushes with death – 'nine lives' – that had begun almost at my birth. At the age of six weeks I required a serious operation – this was in 1934, well before the discovery of antibiotics, when child death was frequent. But I was fortunate to have a caring mother of great competence, who saw me through the post-operative difficulties.

Another example of her abilities was when she was driving our Austin 7, in the days before safety belts, let alone child seats and, playing with the door-opening mechanism, I fell out while we were driving at some 20 miles per hour. My mother had the quickwittedness

As a baby

to seize my ankle as I disappeared out of the now open door and all I suffered from was scratches on my left hand, which had trailed in the gravel before she pulled me up. I had the scars for decades afterwards.

Soon after my birth my parents decided to move to the seaside, despite the threat of aggression from a Germany governed by the National Socialist Party led by Hitler.

My parents on a courtship journey to Devon; and on their wedding day

They were looking for somewhere from where my father could still be able to get to his city job in less than an hour. They chose Leigh-on-Sea, which at that time was a small port but adjacent to the beaches at Chalkwell and Westcliff-on-Sea. It was the first summer we were there that brought about the third of my 'nine lives'. With my mother on the beach I wandered off, as I was prone to do, walked down the jetty at Chalkwell, slipped on

some seaweed and fell into about ten feet of water. Of course at that age I couldn't swim. As I sank down and the light from the surface grew dimmer, I somehow instinctively clutched at some underwater steps which I suppose fishermen used during the lower tides, and I managed to climb back out. Meanwhile another little boy who had been with me, had rushed off to my mother shouting "He's fallen in the water!" She asked everyone in the vicinity if they'd seen me. Fortunately some people had spotted a dripping three-year-old and pointed her in my direction.

Our first stay in Leigh-on-Sea was short-lived because, when I was five, the Second World War started. I can remember my

Bawleys – cockle boats – on Leigh Creek, some of which went to Dunkirk

mother and I sitting on the beach at Chalkwell, seeing the little ships straggling back from Dunkirk.

One of the fishermen from Leigh-on-Sea was killed and after the war, a fishing boat built for Leigh was named *The Boy David* after the young man who'd lost his life. A few weeks after Dunkirk, people living in coastal areas which might be invaded by the Germans were moved away inland. My parents chose to go to Reigate in Surrey, where my mother's family were and where my father had spent much of his early youth.

My mother's father, Ernest, was a wonderful man. He had fought in the First World War in France as an artilleryman and, although a mile or so behind the front line, had been gassed as the gas from German shells blew from east to west across the line.

**Grandpa Ernest Jupp
in his Royal Artillery uniform**

He somehow survived but had a weak chest for the rest of his life.

Such was the employment situation after the First World War that he had to take a job as a Prudential insurance premium collector, in the days when the insurance industry was sustained by collections at front doors. He was a social person and people loved his calling, when they could exchange local gossip. The work required him to be outside in all weathers and his weak lungs suffered as a consequence of rainy days. However, he remained cheerful and was the ideal grandfather. Whenever I was staying at his home, if things got difficult between him and his wife and daughters, he would seize the hand of this five-year-old and say "Us men must stick together." Then he'd take me down to his refuge in the garden: a greenhouse where he grew his beloved tomatoes. He taught me a lot besides how to prick out tomato buds, showing me more about the world than school did. He was interested in knowledge for its own sake and he allotted some of his hard-earned cash to subscriptions to Arthur Mee's *Children's Encyclopedia* and the *National Geographic* magazine. With his help I was given an insight into world affairs and scientific

"Us men must stick together"

discovery, an interest in which remains with me until today. He always answered my questions when he could or, with me, looked up answers in the encyclopedia. It was a joyful upbringing during the Second World War when my own father was away and my mother was working. I would spend school holidays with my grandparents and the chores which were required were a delight – things like going to the fish and chip shop on the corner and bringing home two pieces of fish and sixpenny worth of chips,

which would provide a positive feast for my grandparents and me. Food was rationed in very small quantities and I can remember going to the Co-op, which was next door to the fish and chip shop, and getting the tiny pat of butter that rations allowed, along with ounces of sugar, and bringing them back home to my grand-mother. The only fruit and vegetables we had were grown in my grandfather's garden, or received in exchange for some of his produce. There was a small amount of meat in our diet: two adults and a child could have enough beef in the ration to produce a miniature

Grandma Jupp (centre), my mother (right) and my aunt Vera

Sunday roast. One of the things that we had as pudding was junket, a milk-based dish made with rennet, that could be accompanied by plums or apples from the garden. All in all, it was possibly

Preparing for war in Reigate

the healthiest diet I've had in my life.

My early awareness of world affairs may have come from my grandfather, but my mother continued to develop it, following the progress of the war with me. We had maps on the morning room wall and I painted little paper flags, which we moved as the armies advanced or retreated.

I had been born on the 30th November 1934, which was Churchill's 60th birthday. The nation began to celebrate his (and my) birthday every time victories occurred around that date. Sadly, when the nation rejected Churchill in favour of a Labour government in 1945, the celebrations on my birthday ceased. But one final tailpiece to the

wartime relationship occurred as I sat outside my front door on Wimbledon Common on my 40th birthday in 1974. I heard the unmistakeable sound of a supercharged Merlin engine, which had been the driving force of the Spitfires that helped us win the Battle of Britain. I looked up and saw the familiar shape as it passed above the Common. It was a very emotional moment,

With my father in the early war years

the sound and sight connecting me with my wartime childhood. It turned out to have been a lone Spitfire that had flown over Whitehall to celebrate the centenary of Churchill's birth.

The war period upset the lives of many, but my parents' decision to go back to the family heartland of Reigate had been a sensible one. My mother was able to earn some money working for an insurance company that was within walking distance of our house at Shaw's Corner. Meanwhile her sister Vera, "my favourite aunt" – "I am your **only** aunt," worked for the Admiralty and became quite senior when the Admiralty was itself evacuated to Bath. At the end of the war she was so well thought-of that she and I were granted a place in the Admiralty window overlooking the Cenotaph for the Victory Parade.

During the war she used to come back to Reigate for a break from time to time and it was on one of these occasions that my fourth brush with death took place. Vera was looking after her husband's dog, a cross between a Bull Terrier and an Alsatian. My uncle Frank had left it with her when he was sent abroad with the Reconnaissance Corps. My mother and her sister were walking in the pouring rain on Reigate Hill and in my usual adventurous way I had gone down an almost vertical chalk slope and was crossing it in mountaineering style. But the wet chalk was like slippery grease and my feet began to lose their grip. Vera and my mother were talking but Rex the dog noticed that I was in danger. He placed himself between me and what was a sheer drop of a 100 feet or so, and prevented an impending disaster. Vera and my mother finally noticed that I was in trouble, though I didn't recognise it as such, and they lowered a large branch which had fallen off one of the trees that autumn. They told me to hang on to it and together these two doughty ladies hauled me up. Rex followed, keeping between me and the drop all the way back to safety. I have been a dog lover ever since.

I'd gone down a steep chalk slope. The dog placed himself between me and a 100 foot drop

Canadian troops were garrisoned in Reigate prior to the unwise adventure of the Dieppe raid in France – another of Churchill's sometimes mad ideas. Vera's husband Frank was the most wonderful naughty uncle a boy could want. He was undoubtedly an asset to his unit in the Army when he got to north Africa. While he was in England he came home to Reigate from an exercise in the Surrey countryside with one or two spare explosive 'thunderflashes' in his knapsack. Slightly the better for beer one night, he lit a thunderflash and threw it down from the balcony of the flat in which we were staying. There was a colossal explosion and the garrison was turned out by their duty officer to combat what they clearly thought was the beginning of an invasion. Reigate was suddenly full of hundreds of Canadian troops with ready-loaded guns, looking to use them on the German invaders. There could have been a tragic consequence but in fact all that happened was my uncle asked me to hide him in my cot under the stairs and the Canadians returned to barracks. Quite how Frank avoided being put 'on a charge' one will never know, but he was a man of great charm. Sadly, in north Africa he was killed not by enemy fire, but by being thrown off the back of his Bren Gun Carrier as it went over a steep sand dune. I helped look after his dog Rex until the end of the war.

CHAPTER THREE

Essex boy

Wearing the Radnor House school uniform

My father had a major influence on my education. That influence started in the usual way: I was sent to the prep school that he'd been to. This was Radnor House school on the northern edge of Redhill Common. It was run by two sisters, the Rougiers, who had set up the school just before my father went to it. By the time I got there the masters had been sent off to the Second World War and the Rougiers had been asked to stay on, even though they were getting a bit old and frail. Despite my father's good intentions, my education around the age of 11 was somewhat disturbed and I failed Common Entrance. One of my excuses for this might be that this was the time when the 'doodlebugs' (V1 unmanned flying bombs) were arriving in the skies above Britain. They had a distinctive engine noise which none of us had ever heard before, but we quickly learned that when that noise stopped they were on the way down to explode on some unfortunate. While I was taking the

Fees are payable in advance. The usual Term's notice or a Term's payment is required before the removal of a Pupil.

Termly Fees.

Boarders (including Laundry)	29	guineas
Weekly Boarders	25	,,
Day Boys	7	,,
Day Boys under 10 years of age	5	,,
Morning Attendance, under 6 years	3½	,,
Dinners for Day Boarders (5 per week)	3	,,

A concession in Fees is allowed for Brothers, also for Boarders who are under 9 years of age.

A small Fee is charged for Stationery and the use of Text Books.

Optional.

Piano or Violin	2 guineas	Carpentry	½ guinea
Solo Singing	2 guineas	Boxing	½ guinea
Riding (by arrangement).		Swimming	½ guinea

Radnor House fees at the time

exam I could see out of the corner of my eye one of these descending and exploding on Reigate Hill. This was not their real target, but the reasons they were falling on Reigate included not just that they were being shot at and damaged by English anti-aircraft fire or fighters, but they were being built by forced labour in Germany (Poles, Russians etc) who were busy sabotaging the bombs before they even took off. One of the damaged bombs descended on the outskirts of Reigate itself, blowing down the side of a house, complete with a lady who was having a bath who flew straight out of the bathroom, still in the bathtub, and landed in the road. Incredibly she survived. There were many miraculous escapes during the Second World War, but that was one of the more unusual survivals.

My father had been taken off the Reserved Occupations list, which he had been on because of his role in the running of the Port of London. The port had been largely destroyed in the Blitz, so many previously-restricted jobs were now derestricted and he was called up to the Royal Artillery in time to join a unit that formed part of the air defences of the UK. The V1s were posing a new air threat to Britain and my father's unit was one of the many deployed in south-east England with the intention of stopping them before they did any damage. Despite this, some did get through. My father was variously stationed in south-east Essex (his prewar home ground) and the south coast. He referred to his postings as "the Nesses", Shoeburyness and Dungeness. When he was demobilised in 1946, to his eternal credit he made it his first priority to give me the chance that had been taken from him at the beginning of the First World War, of a standard education at an English public school. But clearly, if I wasn't bright enough to pass

My father's Dollar Academy rugby cap

Common Entrance, he was going to have an uphill struggle. At the beginning of the First World War my father had been taken away from Sevenoaks public school in Kent to Dollar Academy in Scotland – an excellent school, but 12 hours' train ride away in Clackmannanshire. The reason for this upheaval was that his father was German – a type designer, who was brought over to England before the First World War by The Monotype Corporation to join their talented design team. The family still went by their German name, Steltzer. German names became a terrible liability when war broke out in 1914 and my grandfather and his wife were interned in a camp on the Isle of Man. Fortunately, before long old Fritz Max, who quickly dropped the names Fritz and Steltzer, was rescued by the chief designer from Monotype, Stanley Morison, who had told the

My paternal grandfather, Fritz Max Steltzer

Minister for Information that if he wanted good, clear headlines in the press, then Monotype needed Max back in the office. My grandfather changed his surname from Steltzer to his wife's maiden name of Bonner and they returned to Reigate, which was close to Monotype's headquarters.

Perhaps as a result of these experiences, my father read avidly about education. He became aware, in the late years of the wartime coalition, that the Minister for Education,

R A Butler, was introducing a bill (the 1944 Education Act) that would allow parents of limited income to get a grant from their local authority to send promising pupils to public schools. You no longer had to take an exam to get in, but had to pass an interview. We were now back living in Essex and Essex County Council had a particular relationship with a school called Felsted, which had just moved back to the area from being evacuated to Herefordshire and needed more pupils. Thus it was that, via my father's efforts and an enlightened local authority, I passed the interview and was able to take a place at Felsted, a boys' public school, in the autumn of 1947.

1947 was one of the coldest years of the century and the school, like every other institution, had a minimal fuel ration. We spent a lot of time wrapped up in heavy clothing, or hugging radiators for the few hours that they were actually turned on. What's more, the school was on a hill – the only substantial hill in Essex. There was a story about the legendary headmaster, the Reverend Bickersteth, taking the parents of some prospective new boy around. When the mother said "It must be very cold here in winter," the headmaster pulled himself up to his full height and said "Madam, it is never cold here, it is bracing." The memory of running cross-country with my running shoes cracking the icy surface of puddles lives with me to this day.

At Felsted I was able to play rugby (at my prep school I had only played soccer) and, indeed, I went to have special rugby coaching at the Central Council for Physical Recreation at Bisham Abbey in Buckinghamshire. In the summer I was hopeless at cricket but did some athletics, notably high jump and shot put. At the age of 16, with my background at Leigh-on-Sea, I thought that the school ought to have a sailing club. Together with a boy who had a boat at West Mersea, I persuaded one of the masters who was keen on sailing,

**Representing Felsted in the
Essex Schools Athletics competition**

Michael Mann, to support us in setting up a team. Normally it might have been difficult to introduce a new sport, but since the Daily Telegraph Public Schools' Sailing Championships, held by the Royal Corinthian Yacht Club at Burnham-on-Crouch, took place during the summer holidays, Michael Mann was able to get the general support of the school. Our whole team had relevant experience sailing off the Essex coast and so were familiar with the waters of the Crouch.

There were some talented members of my team, including David Powell, who later was to skipper the winning yacht in the Sydney Hobart race, and Roger Pipe, who became an Olympic single-handed sailor. So we did win more than a few races. Alas, after I left, the riotous behaviour of public school boys (not necessarily Felstedian) at the Championships meant that the Corinthian Club decided it could not go on supporting them.

There were Parents' Days at Felsted. One over-generous father lent his car to Howard Leaman, one of my housemates. It was a great privilege in those days to be able to take the test and drive a vehicle. So we all piled into his father's car and drove off to the nearest market town, Chelmsford. As Howard drove us over a crossroads – which did not have a sign saying which road had right of way – another vehicle crashed into the side of our car. Miraculously it didn't roll over but the collision was so violent that the people sitting on the left-hand side of the car were quite seriously injured, with broken bones and concussion. I only suffered bruises, but it could have been very much worse. In effect, it was the sixth of my nine brushes with death.

My first year at Felsted had been a bit of a shock. It was a tougher milieu than I'd known in Reigate. Not only was there the cold of the Essex countryside, but also there was a certain amount of bullying – particularly from one prefect, who clearly enjoyed beating young boys. There was one other factor that was strange to someone new to public school, which was sex. All adolescents go through massive changes in their hormone balance and start to see themselves in relation to other boys, when the younger boy may be found attractive by those older than him. These feelings could get really very intense. I was a stranger to this world, no such emotional factors having existed at my previous school. The interesting discovery was that one had great friendships that were nothing to do with emotions, but were founded on sport and other male obsessions, and yet with another boy there could be a quite deep emotional attachment. The former sorts of male bonds were the kind that lasted into adulthood, whereas for me the emotional component proved to be a passing phase.

By the time I was in my second year I felt thoroughly at home at Felsted and was

On the way to tennis, in white shorts

enjoying some success at sport, as well as comic behaviour such as imitating masters which, as many schoolboy memoirs have described, is the way to deflect unwelcome attention of the bullying kind.

There were various extensions to contact with school friends during some of the holidays, away from the hierarchy of the public school. One of the masters had the idea of getting a free skiing trip for himself by taking some of us on a Thomas Cook skiing package. For schoolboys in the post-war austerity period to go to Europe was an excitement, even if we only had very little foreign currency to spend. But I, and several people I've met since those days, remember changing trains at Basle to go up via Interlaken to Adelboden, where the ski school that we were to attend was based. To have real coffee, croissants — which we'd never seen before — wonderful Swiss butter and red cherry jam, in the café on Basle station, was something close to heaven. But some austerity did follow us. In the hotel at Adelboden we not only had to share rooms, which was understandable, but also had to share bath water. The Swiss tendency to thrift, allied to post-war shortages, meant that the fuel to provide hot water was in short supply. I did learn to ski and ultimately got my British Ski Club Bronze Award.

On the slopes at Adelboden

Alas, I never was able to do much more skiing after that, though when many years later I was making a film about Roald Amundsen I found that, as with cycling, skiing was a skill that didn't leave you, even after a gap of many years. Some 20 years later Switzerland was to feature in my life in a major way.

My earliest writing

It was in my latter years at Felsted that my interest in writing and drama found an outlet. The school had two magazines. One was the standard news magazine called *The Felstedian* and the secondary magazine was *The Cromwellian* (so named because Oliver Cromwell's son Richard, 'Tumbledown Dick', had been sent there in the 17th century). *The Cromwellian* was for the poets and other creative writers in the school to express themselves. I ran a little column entitled Miscellany, in which the standard fare was jokey comments on the latest developments in the school. We had substantial grounds and very fertile soil and most of the young groundsmen were sent off on national service, so the headmaster had the brilliant idea that people could opt out of Games one day a week and instead do estate work: pruning, digging etc. My school friends and I were largely incompetent at trimming hedges and digging ditches and I came up with the phrase "when a job badly needs doing, it's done – badly." I also kept an eye on the real world of journalism and when there was a fire in our main hall, I submitted a piece to the *Evening Standard* Londoner's Diary. My report began by quoting the fire instructions displayed in the school, which said 'the assembly in case of fire takes place in the school hall'. I went on to point up the irony of 250 boys assembling in a hall that was already on fire. In fact, we had all assembled on the cricket pitch across the path from the hall. I made my first journalist fee, at the age of 17, of five guineas.

My father offered to frame the cheque! The school motto was 'Garde ta Foy' which, though it actually meant 'Keep to your faith' was translated by most of us in later life as 'Look after your liver'!

Though my other writing did include rather tedious poetry, I was always drawn by the temptation to write comedy. Thus, in one of the end-of-term sketch shows, I pre-dated *The Two Ronnies'* "fork handles" sketch with the following: a 17th-century landowner, splendidly attired in the fashion of the time, is patrolling his estate to check on his workers and he says to one of them who's busy weeding "Well done, my man. Is there anything you need?" "Yes, m'lud, I need new hoes." The landowner said "Oh, do you like what I'm wearing?" "No, sir, but I reckon you could buy several hoes for the price of your stockings." Sadly, I was not able to use such skills for comedy in my professional career.

CHAPTER FOUR

Join the Army and see the world
(and discover that not everybody likes us)

In theory the most dangerous aspect of my young life was my two years' national service in 1953–55. The fact that I got a commission in the Army owed quite a lot to Felsted. The school had a Combined Cadet Force (CCF) unit, where we drilled and went on firing ranges, like young soldiers. I achieved some degree of promotion in the CCF, I think because I was tall and had a loud voice! But it stood me in good stead when, after the 12 weeks' initial training as a private in the Royal Army Service Corps, I went to a War Office selection board at

With the general inspecting the passing out parade, Buller Barracks, Aldershot, 1953

Barton Stacey in Wiltshire. This was full of practical and written tests about all things military, including leadership. I was able to persuade my examiners that I was 'officer material', thereby ensuring a more challenging but enjoyable remainder of my two years' service. I then went on to the Officer Cadet Training Unit in Aldershot at Mons Barracks. I was successful there and was pleased to think I might be showing my father that all his kind efforts to get me to Felsted had paid off. After the training course I was able to invite my parents to my passing out parade, where I was the senior under officer in command of the parade. My father didn't say much, but I could see that the event had given him pleasure.

I ended up in Egypt with a 'cushy' posting to liaise with journalists and broadcasters. However, the first impact when I arrived was the look and smell of poverty and a man shouting at me as I travelled to the transit camp "You like my wife, effendi? She all white inside like Queen Victoria." It did prepare me for a whole different dimension of experience.

My first command in the Suez Canal Zone was a platoon of petrol and diesel oil tankers which supplied the entire northern half of the Canal Zone with fuel for both vehicles and power generation. My drivers, also national servicemen, were brave lads who daily drove out through territory where they could be ambushed at any time. They had escorts in the form of a marine or infantryman in the cab beside them and another vehicle or vehicles in convoy around them but they were still exposed, sitting on hundreds of gallons of explosive liquid.

I didn't have a platoon sergeant because the platoon had previously been a general transport one and the sergeant who commanded it at the time was caught selling Sten guns to the enemy. The guns had been disarmed but they could have been remanufactured and used against us, and Sergeant Haddow had been court martialled and imprisoned in Colchester military jail before I arrived. So I just had three corporals to run the platoon with me. Privately I named them Dopey, Dozy and Sneezy.

The Sten gun was a cheap hand-held machine gun which was easy to manufacture in large quantity, but was very unreliable unless handled with great care. The corporals and I used to take new recruits fresh out from the UK to the local ranges to get used to the eccentricities of the gun. As I had been warned during officer training in Britain, it was very important to tell whoever was firing a Sten gun on the range that, if it stopped, they were under no circumstances to turn round and say "Sir, it's stopped firing," because one of its eccentricities was it would suddenly revive itself and start firing again. As the corporals and I took the latest bunch of recruits onto the range, I repeated my warning and instructed the corporals to keep an eye on the men. Inevitably, towards the end of the firing session one recruit, baffled by the sudden silence of his gun, turned round and said "Sir, it's stopped firing." I dived to the ground, as did the corporals, leaving the recruit rather stunned by what he'd achieved. Fortunately, on this occasion, the gun did not go off but I was very angry, as were the corporals. They suggested that the stupidity of the young man in question should be punished by giving him extra duties, which I left the corporals to define. Three days later, as I passed the latrines in the desert, I could see the recruit carrying out his punishment. I just hoped he'd learned his lesson.

Three days later, passing the latrines, I could see the recruit carrying out his punishment

In addition to the corporals, another threesome was formed by the three Jones in the platoon, who were known either by their Army number or their accent, so there was a 'Taffy Jones', a '439 Jones' and 'Geordie Jones'. One day 439 Jones drove into the car park in the middle of the morning, ashen-faced, and pointed to a bullethole in the windscreen just in front of his head. He was speechless and I got Dopey and Dozy together to go and find where it happened. By this time Jones had told us that it had been on the Treaty Road about 15 miles north of El Kirsh. I asked Jones whether he was recovered enough to show us exactly where, and got Dopey and Dozy to get the Bren gun out of the armoury and put it in the back of a 15cwt truck. So we set off in my jeep, with the truck behind, and Jones, who was beside me, said "I'll shout to you when we're approaching the

place." We drove on and he pointed out where, from the other side of the Sweet Water Canal he thought he'd been shot at. As we approached it there was movement in the bushes. I yelled "There! That's him!" and Dopey opened fire with the Bren gun resting on the side of the truck. Something thrashed round in the bushes and the boys cheered. As they did so a body

2nd Lieutenant Paul Bonner, guarding the British Empire against the infidels

rolled down the sandy slope into the canal. It was a goat! We never did find the Egyptian sniper.

A detachment

One of the more extraordinary incidents during my desert posting was the matter of Captain Osborne's brothel. Captain Osborne was the second in command of the company. My relationship with him had unexpected aspects, one of which was to inspect the detachment of general purpose transport he commanded in Port Said. I learned later that army detachments were notorious for creating a life of their own and in this case Captain Osborne and his NCOs felt they were supplying an essential service.

On a Friday night they brought in some local women to provide for the sexual needs of the British garrison in Port Said. The furniture was sparse – indeed the paymaster's table was one of the well-used horizontal surfaces. My commander back in El Kirsh clearly had been tipped off that something odd was going on in the unit in Port Said and I soon found that several of the troops up there were willing to spill the beans. But what was I to do with the now fairly conclusive proof that Captain Osborne was running a brothel? In the end I thought I would let my company commander reveal how much he knew, so I said to him "Did you know that there were certain strange goings-on in the unit at Port Said? Is that why you sent me there?" He huffed and puffed and finally admitted that if he'd gone to see for himself it would have ended in not just a court martial for Captain Osborne (which happened anyway) but a disgrace for the whole company, whereas if I reported it, it could be the starting point for a whole examination. The enquiry by the military police and the consequences went on for such an age that I never really got to know the final outcome.

Meanwhile back in El Kirsh, there was a quite different crisis in my platoon. Dopey, Dozy and Sneezy were all of limited stature but they knew about engines and vehicles and somehow, but with increasing difficulty, they kept the platoon of aging lorries on the road. This was to bring me another piece of good fortune. One morning none of the vehicles would start, despite the loving care of the corporals. Eventually we got a Royal Electrical and Mechanical Engineers corporal along and he was able to start four vehicles. Because my platoon was the sole

carrier of both petrol and diesel oil, the northern Canal Zone
came near to being immobilised and in darkness. Word got back
to Headquarters British Troops in Egypt and Brigadier
Saunders, responsible for all transport in the northern Canal
Zone, was so stirred by the news that the next morning he
drove up to our camp at El Kirsh to see what was happening.

That morning Dopey, Dozy and Sneezy had done enough to
get a handful of the 24 vehicles away. The brigadier slapped his

**Rugby in the Canal Zone was played on watered-down sand which
became like concrete (Paul Bonner on the left)**

stick on his boots and said to me "I think you've made your point young man. I will get the Ordnance to release another half dozen tankers from Tel-el-Kebir." Having won this concession I accompanied Brigadier Saunders to breakfast at the mess. As we walked he said "What hobbies do you have at the weekend?" I said "I run the company's sports." "Do you sail at all?" asked the brigadier. I, who had my own dinghy at home in Leigh-on-Sea in Essex, was happy to confirm that I actually could. "Good," said Brigadier Saunders. "My crew is about to be demobbed and I'm looking for someone quite substantial to crew for me at the sailing club on Lake Timsah. Could you come down next Saturday?" Duly on the Saturday afternoon I met the brigadier at the officers' club on Lake Timsah where they raced Snipe class dinghies. I climbed aboard and did my best in a race in which his skills made sure we were in the top three places. What he thought of me I'm still not sure, but he said "I think I'd like to use you again next Saturday." We went on to win several races and my position as his crew was confirmed. So that he could have me to talk over race tactics, he found me a position in his office in the HQ British Troops in Egypt. It was extremely tedious, involving shuffling bits of paper, but instead of the noisome deep trench latrines of El Kirsh in Moascar, we had flush lavatories – the height of luxury!

A surprising new role

There were several officers' messes and I was assigned to one that was not associated with any regiment, but was a sort of general melee of other HQ officers. There I met someone else who was to have a major impact on my life, the moustachioed Colonel John Stubbs of the Sherwood Foresters. He learned that I'd done some journalism at school and before joining the Army, and told me he ran the Public Relations Unit of

HQ British Troops in Egypt, looking after visiting journalists and politicians. "We also write 'local boy's stories'," he said and went on to explain "The unit has a photographer and I get him to take a picture of someone in a geographically-located regiment, say the Hampshires. We then write a story about how well the boy is doing and get it published in their local paper back home. That is a 'local boy's story'. See what you can do." Once again I was on trial. I wrote something to go with the photograph of a boy from the Borderers and it was published in the local Carlisle newspaper. That was good enough for Colonel John.

It turned out to be a very interesting job that saw me go all over the Middle East, from Cyprus to Jordan. In the south of Jordan there was a little fishing port, Aqaba, and there the furthest, and quietist, army outpost was the Royal Artillery battery. This was effectively a platoon-strength station which was such a joyous posting that they even issued their own tie, with an embroidered swan – "going on a swan" being Army parlance for a posting that took you away from the hardship side of the Army. While I was there with the photographer shooting pictures of the young national servicemen of the battery, I was invited to the mess night at the tiny officers' mess. Including engineers and an infantry unit there to guard the artillery, there were not more than a dozen of us. The mess night, normally a formal get-together in full dress, was less formal in Aqaba

The person who threw a 7 on the dice would pay for the drinks, the person who threw 14 would choose the mix of drinks and the person who threw 21 would have to drink it

and many outrageous games were played. One of these was '7-14-21'. Played with four dice, the person who threw 7 would pay for the drinks, the person who threw 14 would choose the mixture of drinks and the person who threw 21 would have to drink the mixture. Very early on, the youngest subaltern in the mess got 21 — a wild mix of green Chartreuse, Island malt and gin. Somehow he managed to hold it down and we went on playing. I threw a 7 and paid for a really extraordinary mix devised by the unit adjutant, and the person who threw 21 was the QARANC (Queen Alexandra's Royal Army Nursing Corps) nurse — a matron-like figure, who was well-prepared to swallow the mixture. But the young subaltern staggered up to her and said "Madam, I will consume it for you," which he did and promptly fell flat into her arms and was sick. She looked over his shoulder at me and said "If I'd known he was going to call on my professional abilities, I would have made sure I drank it myself!"

On the way down from Amman to Aqaba

Colonel John and his second-in-command, Major Hugh Campbell, shaped my broader view of the Army. I was also used as Colonel John's 'gofer'. One of the errands I had to run was picking up his wife, Jane Stubbs, when she arrived at Port Said on a families troop ship. I took the colonel's Land Rover, which was driven by an older national serviceman called Hayward — a merchant seaman who'd been caught staying ashore for too long, been picked up by the military police and drafted into the Army. We collected Jane, who to my eyes was positively glamorous. I sat between the licentious soldiery, Hayward, and the colonel's lady. I was astride the gear lever, much to Hayward's amusement every time he changed gear. As we drove down the canal road there were various road blocks, some of them ours and some run by the Egyptians on behalf of the Canal Company, and each time we had to slow down. We were doing this as we neared El Ballah when an enormous Nubian lifted his jalabiya only a few feet from the colonel's wife and revealed a considerable degree of physical endowment. I shrank into my seat. Hayward giggled but, to my astonishment, Jane simply remarked "What a magnificent specimen!"

Before I left El Kirsh for the easier life of Moascar, near to Ismailia, I was going down to Tel-el-Kebir on the border between the Canal Zone and the Delta to pick up the six new tankers that the Brigadier had agreed. I was in my vehicle, driven by Ron Wood (who by pure chance worked for my boat builder in Leigh-on-Sea), with a jeep escort. As we eased our way through one of the many road blocks there was a cracking sound which, from many years in the butts of the shooting ranges of school, I recognised as a shot over my head. I stood up and drew my revolver. My driver Ron told the story, I believe, for many years afterwards "I once got shot at with my officer, he stood up in the seat beside me waving his revolver and when I accelerated to get us away, he fell over backwards. It was like a Buster Keaton movie." However, it really did constitute the seventh of my 'nine lives', though fortunately more comedy than tragedy.

———————

My first link with broadcasting

How did I get to make documentaries for the BBC, let alone crash in a helicopter in the deserts of California? It all started 20 years before in another stretch of desert, El Alamein, in Egypt. My compulsory two years' national service was ending on a high note as a PR officer for Headquarters British Troops in Egypt. I had been sent as one of the first staff to leave the Canal Zone for the Delta, since the riots of 1952 had forced the British back into the Canal Zone. I was to act as the liaison between the military and the broadcasters: BBC, CBS and broadcasters from Australia, New Zealand, India and other members of the British Empire's forces. My job on this occasion was primarily to look after BBC Radio, who were broadcasting the El Alamein opening ceremony live (there was film newsreel but no television coverage in those days). The BBC man in charge of the broadcast was Harry Middleton, the assistant head of Radio Outside Broadcasts. He was responsible for the coverage of race meetings on radio and, what's more, horse racing was one of his prime interests in life, so he was known amongst his colleagues as Harry 'the Horse'.

During the week we were there we toured the nightclubs of Alexandria together, which hadn't seen any English people for four years, and we became good friends. The bar owners of Alexandria were delighted to hear English voices again and even more delighted to take our piastres.

The ceremony itself in which Field Marshal, later Lord, Montgomery opened the El Alamein war memorial,

Field Marshal Montgomery in dress uniform

An Egyptian war cemetery

was deeply moving. The Highland Light Infantry, who were in Egypt at the time, had a band which played the Scottish mourning lament *Flowers of the Forest*, and as we looked out across the desert with its literally thousands of white crosses of the dead, it was difficult to hold back the tears. In the way that PR people and broadcasters have, after the ceremony Harry and I said farewell not expecting to meet again.

Getting home

In January 1955 I was demobilised from the Army, something that I'd been looking forward to but, in the end, I felt rather sad about. Gone was my ordered life; I'd now have to think and decide things for myself! But on the way back to Britain I had a final demand on my military rank. We were flying 50 troops back to be demobilised with me. I had a company sergeant major but no other command structure and the flight would take about 15 hours. The RAF pilot came back to me looking worried, telling me we were going to be flying into a headwind and he would need to touch down at Malta to refuel, including the centre fuel tank which was in the wing above the cabin. After refuelling, taking off and flying for about another two hours there was a very strong smell of petrol in the cabin. I looked at the sergeant major and said "I think we ought to tell the pilot." I struggled up to the cockpit and gave him the news, asking "Is that normal?" He said "No," handed over to his co-pilot and came back with me. He found there was fuel dripping slowly from a leak in the tank into the cabin. "We have to do something fast," he said. "Get your men to remove their boots so they don't make sparks against the metal studs of the floor." So I instructed the sergeant major to go round, rank by rank on one side, and I went down the other, telling the astonished men to remove their boots. We were flying at about 12,000 feet and the heating in the aircraft was, unbelievably, a paraffin-fired system, which had to be turned off. So I had 48 soldiers who were now worrying that they would be demobilised with frostbite.

We finally came in to land, shivering, at RAF Stansted, in a traditional Essex morning mist. Just as we were all thinking we were safely home, it became apparent the airfield had a fault with its blind landing system. Luckily the pilot noticed that he was flying alongside the runway rather than over it and, since it was built for heavy bombers, it was quite long enough for him to sideslip into the landing position. I, who knew a little about flying, heaved a sigh of relief. The soldiers were simply glad that they were within minutes of being warm again, though in fact they had to cross a bit of wet runway in their socks before they got their boots back. Fortunately RAF Stansted, which was a transport command station, had a warm waiting room for the troops to sit in. As far as I know, nobody got frostbite.

Like so many returning servicemen, I discovered that the girl of my dreams, Hilary Padgham, had become engaged to a very good-looking boy called Saxon. I wasn't very competitive at that age so didn't try to disturb their relationship, but for a while I was to regret Hilary's choice of another man while I was away in Egypt. Five years after I returned I was visiting my parents in Leigh-on-Sea and met a cousin of Hilary's called Valerie Ney. We recognised each other and I asked after Hilary. Valerie went rather pale and said "Didn't you know?" "Know what?" I asked. "Hilary died," she said. "She got tuberculosis a year ago and died within six months."

I was shocked because, although this was indeed before TB had been defeated nationally, it was by now fairly rare for somebody to die of the disease. It seemed a tragedy that chance should strike down the beautiful Hilary.

There was another difficult aftermath that clung to me after demobilisation. In the Greek Club in Ismailia, where kitchen hygiene was not a high priority, I had picked up amoebic dysentery which necessitated, for the next two years, always being close to a lavatory. In live broadcasting, this was not easy!

CHAPTER FIVE

Back to 'civvy street'

After I was demobbed it was time to look for employment, not just to earn a living but to find a purpose in life. I wanted to be a journalist but there were no jobs with my local paper, the *Southend Standard*. However I found a job in the PR office of a radio and electronics manufacturer called E K Cole Ltd, known as Ekco, which was based in Southend. I used to prepare cuttings on electronics, radio and TV from the morning papers in time to be on the desks of senior executives when they came in at 9.30am. I became very good at scanning print for key words like 'electronics', 'radio', etc, and there was a young secretary, the daughter of a local printer, who was clever at duplicating the cuttings that I'd chosen to be distributed. By mid-morning we were both exhausted and would sneak off to the canteen. She became my first girlfriend at work. Occasionally national newspapers were interested in something that Ekco were making and the journalist who was writing the Atticus column in *The Sunday Times*, John Pearson, wanted a picture to illustrate an article he was doing about prospecting for uranium in Canada. Ekco made a sort of Geiger counter on a stick, which did just the job. He published the picture and I was praised by my boss for having got a product of ours into *The Sunday Times*. It was the beginning of a lifelong friendship between John Pearson and me.

This is where Harry 'the Horse' Middleton of the BBC was to make his surprise reappearance in my life. In those days, after your two years' national service you had to do reserve training at weekends and with a summer camp. Just before I went away for my training, there was an event called *Radio Olympia*, where manufacturers of radio and the early television exhibited their wares in Kensington. I had to be on E K Cole's stand and I was looking for lunch dates who I knew worked in town. I tried James Cameron of the *News Chronicle*, who I'd helped in Egypt, but he was away around the world somewhere and the next card that came out of my wallet was for Harry 'the Horse'. I rang him at the BBC and he said "Can you have lunch?" I said "When?" He said "Tomorrow." We met at what was then one of the few wine bars in London, Shirreff's, round the corner from the BBC.

I got there first and Harry rushed in, waving a document. It turned out to be an eight-page application form to join the BBC. We sat down and remembered Alexandria, then he laid the form down on the table between us, saying "You must fill this in and return it to me as soon as possible." It asked for everything, down to my grandmother's maiden name. We had a jovial lunch, but he never did tell me why he thought I should apply to the BBC. He muttered something about being a studio manager, which I assumed meant sweeping up after the actors had left the studio. We said a cheery farewell and the next week I went on my Army reserve training to Thetford Forest in Norfolk. One lunchtime our adjutant sought me out, saying "Your

"There's a letter from the BBC. Shall I open it?" said my father. A pause. "It's asking you to go for an interview tomorrow"

father rang. I hope it's not bad news." I decided I'd ring him back in the office, and he said "A letter arrived yesterday with 'BBC' on the envelope, shall I open it?" I said "Yes, but it'll only be to say that my application has been rejected." He opened it and there was a pause, followed by a gasp. He said "It's asking you to go to Broadcasting House tomorrow at two o'clock to be interviewed." I thought quickly and said "Take my de-mob suit to work with you and I'll change in your office and go on from there." I arrived in Broadcasting House just in time for the interview and was horrified to be shown into a room with eight people, all but one men, waiting to interview me. They all asked questions like "Could I read music?" and "Had I done drama at school?" and so on. Later my voice was tested, but the last of the eight looked at me and said "I see you were at Felsted School. What house were you in?" "Windsor's." "So was I," he said, "20 years ago." As I left the room, I thought "If I don't get the chance to work for the BBC after that, I don't think I'll ever get a lucky break."

Going west

Duly, two weeks later, a letter arrived saying I'd got a job as a "Studio Assistant, Trainee" at a salary of £465 p.a. and I could do it in London, Bristol or Belfast. London was too expensive, Belfast, even in those days was a rough posting, so I thought I should choose to be interviewed for a job in Bristol. I went down to the city the day before and fell in love with the place. It was the late summer of 1955 and even though its heart had been bombed during the war, Bristol was still a beautiful city scenically, with skylines and the Mendip Hills visible in the distance from the centre. So by the time I got to Broadcasting House (BH) Bristol in Whiteladies Road, I would have been desperately disappointed had I not been accepted there, at least for the six months' 'probation'. A nice personnel lady fixed me up with a room in theatrical digs within walking distance of BH and I started to learn what in fact turned out to be the basic skills of live broadcasting – primarily timing and concentration.

My BBC career commenced on 5th September 1955 and, as I settled in as the trainee studio assistant I became aware that this was the ideal career for me. I had a talent for writing and, to a certain extent, for the sort of dexterity and timing that broadcasting in those days demanded. But above all, I loved radio and had done since I was a child, so I was in the perfect situation for me to develop, knowing that I wanted to spend my whole life in broadcasting. The other aspect that drew me in was the ethos of the BBC, not just to 'inform, educate and entertain', but the sense of serving the public. That may sound a bit worthy, but I was really filled with pleasure every time I went in to a studio or control room. I knew it was the life for me.

It was wonderful, working with actors and broadcasters on drama programmes like Hardy's *Woodlanders*, with actors like Tony Britton and Renée Asherson, and J B Priestley's *Three Men in New Suits*. In the latter, one of the characters comes back out of the Army and a neighbour shouts that there'd been "American men in the house, some of them black." He goes into his home, finds endless empty gin bottles left by the Americans and goes round throwing the bottles at a stone wall. It was quite difficult to provide the sound effects for that in a small radio studio. I set up a slab of paving stone and all the empty bottles I could get from the BBC Club downstairs, and a sort of canvas screen to stop the glass flying about the studio. In addition the smashes had to be timed to the actors' lines – a demanding task. Somehow I achieved it and got praise both from the producer and my boss. I thought this was the best job I could ever want to have, doing things that were fun and helping actors who I admired.

There was some formal instruction at the training school in Marylebone High Street in London, where we learned about the different microphones for different jobs and, above all, how to create sound effects. An example would be producing a creaking castle door, for which you got some string from the post room, a composition waste paper basket from Office Supplies and cloth and rosin from the music studios. You then threaded the string through the bottom of the waste paper basket and, with your foot on the upside down bin, pulled the rosin cloth up the string. This made a sound just like a creaking door, rounded off by slamming a standalone sound effects door in the studio.

Having successfully survived my six months' probation, I became a fully-fledged studio manager in Bristol in May 1956, and was granted a £50 p.a. pay rise. I was also sent on another course at the BBC Engineering Training School at Evesham. The majority on the course were male studio managers, but there were two women. The men had dormitories in the main building while the women had a separate small building to themselves called Pear Tree Cottage. In charge of the whole establishment was a senior engineer called Dr Sturdy. He had a firm belief that testosterone-driven young men were liable to try to gain entry to visit the girls in Pear Tree Cottage after hours. Most

Bristol, with the Clifton suspension bridge over the Avon

of the men were indeed going there with bottles of cider and crisps for impromptu parties. Dr Sturdy took to patrolling the area and, hearing a suspicious amount of noise, burst in and told us that Pear Tree Cottage was out of bounds to the men. Needless to say, it wasn't long before we returned to partying with the girls. One evening we were all in there when we heard Sturdy's dog bark outside. We dived into cupboards and under beds. Sturdy came in and addressed the girls. "Is everything all right?" Giggling, they of course replied "Yes." I had thrown myself under one of their beds and since they didn't keep a very tidy house, it was quite dusty down there and I couldn't stop myself sneezing. Sturdy's Alsatian bounded underneath the bed and my game was up. From then on, we were not just banned but there were surprise patrols of the staff to check on the cottage. It was not so much Abbott and Costello, more St Trinian's.

My favourite job as a studio manager was to work on the West Region's nightly radio news magazine programme, *Round-Up*. It came after the *Six O'Clock News* on the Home Service and there were lots of last-minute items, delivered on disc with only moments to spare. There was a big adrenalin rush, which pleased me and to which I responded effectively – so effectively that when the editor of the programme was away, the head of Talks in the West Region asked me to edit the nightly programme, giving me the job title of acting assistant producer. By now I had been working in programme-making for three years, during which time I had been doing all the humble but enjoyable tasks of a studio manager. On one occasion I had to fetch a disc from the recording suite, as ever last-minute, and get it on the air before the programme finished. Rushing down the corridor in Whiteladies Road, I knocked over a rather small man. I knew I had to get the disc to the studio in time for instant transmission, so I said to a passing colleague "Pick him up and give him my apologies," dashed into the studio and put the disc on air. Only after the programme ended did I learn that I had knocked down Sir Ian Jacob, the Director General (DG) of the BBC, who was on a visit to Bristol. When I went to apologise to the DG in the controller's office, he was relaxed about it, but the controller seemed to think it was a reflection on his authority.

Fortunately in my first foray into editing Talks programmes, the presenter of *Round-Up* was a very experienced broadcaster who had served in the Forces Broadcasting Unit in Germany. He was called Derek Jones. He had a wonderful voice, a quick mind and infinite patience with young, ambitious studio managers like me, and he taught me a lot. As well as editing the magazine programme from time to time I also produced reports for it, going out on the streets to do what are known as 'vox pops' –

getting the opinions of passers-by – on matters of West Regional significance. To do this you walked around with an enormous box called an EMI Midget tape recorder. It weighed a ton and on a hot day it was something you came to loathe. Being the first of its kind, it also had a lot of idiosyncrasies. One of them was that, although the tape could be driven forward to record, the U2 batteries were not strong enough to wind the tape back at the end of the interview. The reporter had to do this with a little handle that was so ill thought-out to the point where it damaged your fingernails. Though my

A 'vox pop' with a passer-by on his way to work

'vox pops' were usable, most of them weren't very distinctive and I came to prefer being the editor of the programme – setting tasks for wonderful west country contributors such as Charles Causley, a Cornish poet of national status, and Bernard Fishwick, another Cornishman with an eye for a good story.

Although I was only an acting assistant producer, I had a certain standing within the Bristol media community. I regularly

Interviewing six Commonwealth bishops with the so-called Midget recorder

joined the editors of the *Western Daily Press* and the *Evening Post* at the Portcullis pub opposite the Grand Spa Hotel in Clifton on a Sunday lunchtime to chew over local affairs, particularly the media and arts. Through these connections I came to know the casts and directors of the Bristol Old Vic Theatre and the Little Theatre and became part of the group that sat at the actor Peter O'Toole's feet in his flat in Clifton — a haunt of arts correspondents and other hangers-on. I found that a young man sitting cross-legged behind me was called Tom Stoppard, at that time the theatre critic of the *Western Daily Press*. Peter O'Toole was the leader of the pack, as it were, and his talent was already evident. He played a brilliant Jimmy Porter in one of the early productions of John Osborne's *Look Back in Anger*, and an actress called Wendy Williams played Alison, his much put-upon wife. Bristol in those days was a wonderful place in which to be a part of the city culture. In many ways I would have liked to have spent my whole life there but the nature of the development of broadcasting, and my restless ambition, determined otherwise.

It was in Bristol that I met my wife-to-be. Jenifer Hubbard had been a secretary to the first female producer of *Woman's Hour* in London, but her parents lived outside Bristol. When her eldest sister was found to suffer from multiple sclerosis, Jeni returned to Bristol to help the family. She applied for a job at BBC Bristol and was immediately taken on. The producer she worked for was addicted to golf. He was the West Region's producer for the Overseas Service and he used to leave material for the half hour programmes for me, in his absence, to put together for transmission. Interviews that he did with people from abroad were compiled on discs, which at the time were the recording medium, before tape had been taken into use by the BBC. It was left to Jeni and me to get the programme on the air. I, as studio manager, operated the bank of playback turntables, dashing from 15 seconds on one disc to 25 on another, and changing the first disc for a third one. Meanwhile Jeni controlled the very variable sound levels as each new recording was played, requiring constant vigilance so as not to blow the transmitters off the air – which was allegedly what happened if the sound levels went over the figure six on the peak programme meter. At the end of all this, we were both so drained that we tended to fall into each other's arms.

This reaction to our work became a warm relationship, which was enhanced by her remarkable family, who one could have described as 'characters' – quite different from the suburban conformity which had surrounded me in Leigh-on-Sea.

With Jeni, newly engaged, at her Uncle Wallace's asparagus farm

Within a few months we became engaged and we married in July 1956.

We enjoyed getting away to have a good meal in one of the burgeoning crop of restaurants which, as wartime austerity began to fade, had aspirations towards fine dining and even an entry in the newly-launched *Good Food Guide*. We also enjoyed playing squash and tennis together. Meanwhile, Jeni introduced me to all sorts of aspects of culture which she understood and I didn't. For instance, the limit of my understanding of classical music was my mother's passion for Grieg and my discovery in a school music class of Beethoven's *Symphony No. 7*. I had regarded composers like Mahler and Bruckner as being tuneless monsters. But listening with Jenifer to recordings, or the Proms on the radio, I gradually began to learn from her tastes the joys of the more complex composers. In those days the BBC still sought to give its employees access to serious cultural events and later, when we came to live in London, we used to get tickets to the Promenade concerts and the two of us went to many of them each season. There was one moment that is so etched in my memory that even now, thinking about it, I feel a welling-up of emotion. Jacqueline du Pré, the great English cellist, had been recorded playing Elgar's *Cello Concerto* in a performance that is still regarded as the finest. Sadly, multiple sclerosis cut short her wonderful interpretation of works for the cello. Jeni and I were at one particular concert when du Pré was in the audience in her wheelchair, on the platform above the stalls reserved for disabled people. The Israel Philharmonic Orchestra, conducted by Zubin Mehta, was playing Elgar's *Enigma Variations*. Mehta paused before the wonderful *Nimrod* and we all found ourselves looking up at the platform and Jacqueline du Pré. With those melancholy notes, written in praise of a friend of Elgar's, there were few people in the Albert Hall who did not shed a tear. Jeni and I were certainly two who did. That was perhaps the greatest moment of emotion gifted to me in my time at the BBC.

Changing times

This period was a time of change in Britain when the old morality was being eroded by new freedoms. Young people had a little more money than their parents, at the same age, and could go on holidays together without parental supervision. This easing of constraints allowed relationships to flourish on the young people's own terms. Added to that, for the educated young, reliable contraception was now a possibility and this again facilitated the new morality. Ultimately the factors of money and contraception in Britain led to what became known as the 'swinging sixties'.

With Jeni and our first-born, Neil. And our first marital home, in Bristol: three living rooms, three bedrooms – and all for £11,000!

In the BBC, as always bound to reflect the changes in wider society, there was a particular interest in sexual freedom, partly because it had quite an impact on the storylines of drama, and even comedy, on television. But also internally in the BBC the plethora of small offices, dressing rooms and other potentially private spaces facilitated the temptations that privacy could provide. It was no longer 'hanky-panky' behind the bicycle sheds!

Meanwhile, for the majority of people, there was a desire to create a stable relationship and a family. Like so many wives,

Jenifer was the hub of the family and ours grew to consist of two boys and a girl. The business of television demanded odd hours of work and/or journeys to locations far from home, so much responsibility fell on the 'broadcasting wives'. Jenifer was brilliant at the task. Neither she nor I wanted our children to go away to boarding school, so a lot of the job of bringing them up fell to her. Inevitably there were dramas in the family. Early on, our second son Mark, when only a few months old, got scarlet fever and had a temperature of 105° F (40.55°C).

Fortunately our doctor lived in a house which backed on to ours. When we rang he heard something urgent in Jeni's voice and made the decision to leap over the back wall and come and attend to our child, who was indeed very ill. With the help of the then relatively new antibiotics and Jeni's care, little Mark recovered and went on to become a strong rugby-playing schoolboy.

Our first big family home, on Wimbledon Common

The children all had different talents. Neil, our eldest son, was one of nature's engineers, always damming streams and building things. Mark had a passion for theatre, not as an actor but as part of the back stage teams. Alison, our only daughter, managed to combine a talent for the classics with sporting prowess that took her to Seoul for the 1988 Olympics as part of the coxless pairs rowing team.

Neil and Mark were born

while we were in Bristol and when I was offered a job in London we had to find somewhere for us all to live. I was attracted to the south-west of the capital, where there were green spaces like Richmond Park and Wimbledon Common. After a difficult period in a very small house (it had won a Scandinavian design award for high-density living!) we were able to find an old Victorian house on Wimbledon Common. It was going very cheaply because other buyers had been put off by the fact it had sitting tenants, who had certain rights of tenure. I was the first person to have actually asked the tenants if they wanted to stay. It so happened that one had been the wife and the **The two women** other the secretary of a man who had lived **couldn't stand the** with them in the house as a 'ménage à trois'. **sight of each other** He had died and the two women couldn't stand the sight of each other, so were willing to move if we gave them time to find alternative accommodation. We remained in this house for the best part of 50 years.

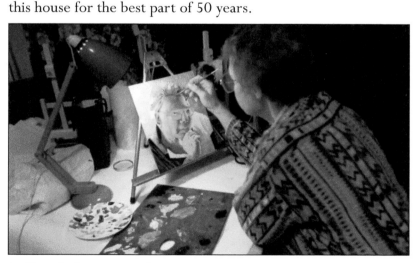

Jenifer painting my portrait

Once the children were at school Jenifer's talents, other than for bringing up the family, began to appear. She became an accomplished artist and sculptor and she started up, with a partner, a small shop in Wimbledon Village High Street selling

dress lengths of material that she had bought cheaply from
Liberty's warehouse in Merton Abbey Mills. She made a modest
profit – but the shop also provided a drop-in stop for the
children on their way home from school and it became
a sort of social centre for the wives of Wimbledon.

Jeni

CHAPTER SIX

Learning the trade

I had first been sent to London by the BBC on what was called an 'attachment', to learn the wider role of a studio manager. This involved working from Broadcasting House in Light Entertainment in studios scattered around London due to the wartime dispersal, including the Paris Cinema in Piccadilly, Aeolian Hall and 200 Oxford Street. Another favourite attachment was to the Overseas Services in Bush House in the Aldwych. Because it housed various language services, it had developed the widest range of cuisines of any canteen in the whole of the BBC.

My happiest attachment was to Light Entertainment. I was overjoyed to be asked to work on one of my favourite shows from my school days – *The Goon Show* – as a junior 'spot effects' man. In Light Entertainment, as in Drama, some of the sound effects were pre-recorded, but some took place live.

On *The Goon Show* the live effects, carried out by a very experienced studio manager, Ron Belchier, were so entertaining that Peter Sellers and Spike Milligan, two of the stars of the show, complained because the audience were applauding the effects. I found that before I arrived, a curtain had been put up between Ron and the audience so they never knew how he achieved the effects and the laughter was reserved for the performers. The comedians Harry Secombe, Peter Sellers and Spike Milligan all had their sensitivities and what might have seemed a minor issue of timing or tone was a matter of great seriousness for them, contrasted with the final effect for the audience, which was usually wonderfully comic.

Another revelation to me was when I was working on dramatised features in radio. I was doing the effects on a feature produced by a well-known and revered producer, Lance Sieveking. After the first run-through I felt a hand at my elbow and the voice of Lance in my ear said "Darling, could you make that door more like a brown leaf falling?" I was left wondering what he had in mind, but I closed the door more quietly next time and Lance seemed to be content with that.

"Darling, could you make that door more like a brown leaf falling?" whispered Lance in my ear

I returned to Bristol as a properly qualified studio manager and was allowed for the first time to attempt music balance. My boss, George Pagan, thought I should start learning about this on 'a nursery slope' and he let me do a one-microphone balance of an organ recital by the young Simon Preston, in St Mary Redcliffe church. Musical instruments had to be clearly heard in a way that the composer intended. George could read music perfectly. I had only a choirboy's skill, which meant I could follow the top line of a music sheet, but tended to lose sight of the other instruments. The organ recital was a late night regional-only programme and so I couldn't do much damage. I walked up and down the aisle with the microphone until the very experienced Outside Broadcast engineer who they'd sent with me said he thought I'd hit the right spot. The usual routine of flashing cue lights to me from Broadcasting House, and from me to Simon, took place and the broadcast worked perfectly.

This led George Pagan to think I could advance a little further in music-balancing experience and, after watching him on a broadcast by the West of England Light Orchestra (WELO), he entrusted me with a subsequent WELO music balance for

Workers' Playtime on my own. The music studio was in fact an old cinema that had been destroyed by fire in the Blitz, but whose walls remained and produced a surprisingly good acoustic. One of the other studio managers had discovered that you could add echo to WELO's strings in a manner that helped them to sound lush. This was achieved by putting a microphone at the top of the concrete fire escape stairs and a loudspeaker at the bottom. To add echo to anything, you switched the signal for that particular part of the orchestra, or singer, through the loudspeaker at the bottom of the fire escape and added the sound that the microphone picked up at the top. Come the day of my first live broadcast music balance, there had been a slight change in the situation. When I faded up the echo from the strings on rehearsal it sounded fine. I swelled with pride. After the red light had gone on and we were broadcasting live, I faded up the famous *Workers' Playtime* signature tune, after which we went into *Greensleeves* as the opening piece. The arrangement for this used all the first and second violins of WELO. As they struck up, I faded in a little echo and was horrified to hear the mass chirping of birds. Unbelievably, during the 'line-up' period between rehearsal and transmission, a flock of starlings had flown through a ventilator shaft and were screaming to get out just as I faded up the echo. I was never allowed to do music balance again.

The BBC West of England Light Orchestra, and 'the sound of chirping starlings'

The BBC embraces ambidexterity

In one of the BBC's senior executive decisions it became policy that, to save bringing in extra staff, radio studio managers should also be working in television as vision mixers, and radio

BBC television directors' course
Back row: Gerard Victory (far left), Paul Bonner (centre)
Front row: James Plunkett Kelly (far left), Julia Smith, co-creator of
EastEnders **(centre), Kevin Billington (right), Peter Wright (far right)**

producers should be able to direct television. This required
a lot of training to achieve the conversions. Most of us in fact
learned on the job.

I did finally get a place on the formal television directors'
course in London. My fellow trainees were a distinguished
crowd: Peter Wright, who later became a brilliant choreographer
with the Royal Ballet; Kevin Billington, who went on to become
a very able feature film director; and, most extraordinary of all,
two Irishmen, James Plunkett Kelly, the novelist, and Gerard
Victory, director of music for Ireland's national broadcaster
RTÉ. The latter two were told by Gunnar Rugheimer, who was
overseeing their training from Ireland, that they'd got to learn
as much as they could about broadcasting by taking the rest of
the course members out for a drink every evening – provided
we were only bought Guinness!

Live television usually involved cutting between three cameras,
which was all we had then, on the command of the director.

As vision mixer, my role was to press the buttons that selected the cameras. Problems arose when the directors, often converted radio producers of a certain age who didn't understand about the 'grammar' of television, would get the cameras set up so that people appeared to be talking to the back of one another's heads. This was known as 'crossing the line'. As a vision mixer who was also an amateur photographer, I could see the problem, so would gently correct by cutting to the required camera, regardless of what the director said. Usually they were quite grateful and so it was I learned the art of camera direction from the vision mixer's desk.

My 'nursery slope' for direction was the regional magazine programme *View of the South and West*. I was always looking for items that we could cover. In London I'd been an enthusiast for traditional jazz and often went to the 100 Club in Oxford Street, where Humphrey Lyttelton and Chris Barber played. Back in Bristol there was a jazz band that regularly played a pub in the Horsefair, led by a clarinettist, Acker Bilk. He was very good both on his instrument and as a leader of the band, so I persuaded my producer Ron Webster that he was worth ten minutes on the show. I asked Acker what he wanted to play on television and he chose *Corinne Corinna*. I dutifully got the 45 rpm disc of his recording out of the library and played it several times while working out the camera shots that I would use. When it came to rehearsal it turned out that, as a director, I thought I could run when I could barely walk. None of the shots worked and I went down onto the studio floor to say to Acker "You're not playing it like your recording." He replied "This is jazz, man, we play it differently every time."

"You're not playing it like your recording," I said. "This is jazz, man, we play it differently every time," said Acker

Rather shamefaced, I worked out that if I shot the whole band on a wide angle on one of the cameras, I could use the other two for close-ups on the band members as they each played. However, anticipating who was going to play next was a bit difficult and more than once I was left with a shot of Acker or his trumpeter busily shaking out the spit from their instruments rather than performing! "Call yourself a director?" asked the producer afterwards. I licked my wounds and returned to the fray. In the end, with Ron's help, I became a pretty good live director. Acker Bilk went on to be a national figure with hit recordings like *Stranger on the Shore*.

I saw television production as a much more complex challenge than radio. In fact in my later years, I came to prefer the subtlety of radio, but in my youth television production delivered an adrenalin rush which I enjoyed. But one had to start in television production in the junior role of a researcher.

CHAPTER SEVEN

The lady on the train

After the excitement of the television directors' course in London, I went back to Bristol at the beginning of 1959 — not returning to Radio but to their Television department, which had only been going for two years. One of my roles was as researcher for a network series on the history of aviation, *The Flying Years*, with a famous man who lived in the west country, Sir Alan Cobham. Sir Alan had done some of the early pioneering flying expeditions to Africa and Australia but, needing to find ways to make money, he decided to develop a route to India and back. On his return he landed his floatplane on the Thames beside the Houses of Parliament and there was film of him running up the steps to the terrace. When he was met later by the Foreign Secretary Lord Halifax he was expecting to be congratulated, but Halifax said "You've just destroyed the whole system of international diplomacy. We used to send letters to India knowing that we wouldn't get a reply for at least eight days, possibly longer. Now we're getting them back in 24 hours. That is not an advance!" But Cobham had lived an adventurous life, was always short of money and welcomed the thought of publicising the company he was setting up on BBC Television. The company, which he named Flight Refuelling, created a special valve which allowed a pipe running from one aircraft with fuel on it, to one running on nearly empty, thus almost doubling the range of the aircraft. This was welcomed by civil transport but particularly by the military, flying long-range bombers. Flight Refuelling was a successful company and at last Cobham was wealthy, but he still had an ego, which allowed us to use him and his adventures on screen. He had a lot of famous aviation friends like Lord Brabazon and F J Camm, who designed the Hurricane fighter. He was a terribly bad presenter and there was no teleprompting at that time, but somehow I got film from the Shell Film Unit and the British Film Institute and we were able to record his voice off-camera to go behind the film. My time was divided between this work and directing, live in the studio, the weekly magazine programme *View of the South and West*. On the latter I found that I really had learned how to 'drive' a studio on the directors' course in London. One of the crew members was kind enough to remark that I now had rather more idea of what directing was about than I'd had when he'd worked with me previously.

Television expands

At about this time the BBC was in the midst of having one of its fits of wanting to fill more hours of television than it had people or studios in London to produce. In Bristol we therefore used to take visiting productions, usually but not always, of programmes for women or children. One of the children's ones was *All Your Own*, a highly-regarded programme in which young people demonstrated their skills – everything from singing to model-making, fronted by an ex-Festival of Britain PR man, Huw Wheldon, who had a wonderful way with words. In our Bristol television studio he was interviewing a boy who had built a model with matchsticks of St Mary Redcliffe church, which Queen Elizabeth I had called "the fairest church in all my land." As Huw talked to camera, I could see in a different camera focused on the model that Huw was squeezing its base and that the spire was about to topple. So I said to the floor manager "For goodness sake get him to put it on the table, otherwise he'll destroy the boy's life's work." The message was duly relayed and St Mary Redcliffe, in all its matchstick glory, survived. This event was to have a quite extraordinary benefit to me in the longer term.

Once at the end of a long day in London tracking down film for *The Flying Years*, I staggered to Paddington carrying a pile of cans of film, only to find that the train to Bristol had been derailed on its way into the station. After a prolonged wait a new train was found, but all the seats originally reserved were now no longer valid and there were battles in compartments as people claimed places. As I fought to get a window seat, the doughtiest fighter for it was a little woman in a funny hat. She would have got that prize seat, even if I hadn't been gracious enough to give it to her. We started to talk and I realised

Grace Wyndham Goldie

I'd met her somewhere before. It turned out she was the assistant head of the old Television Talks department, Grace Wyndham Goldie, and as we talked it became apparent that she was keen on an idea that my wife and I had, which was to use television to separate the good quality from the bad in household products. An organisation had been set up by the sociologist Michael Young to test products and to distinguish between the reliable and unreliable. It was called the Consumers' Association. My wife was keen on the idea and I outlined it to Grace. She was thoroughly in favour, provided the tests of the product were reliable and defensible against any protest from manufacturers. Out of that chance meeting came the idea for a series called *Choice*. We did a pilot programme which was one of the most boring I've ever made, consisting of endless refrigerators, their brand names and their prices. In fact, it was a breakthrough by the BBC, which had never allowed the showing of brand names and prices of products and certainly never, as we now do, naming ones that were dangerous or shoddy. At the recording of the programme, Grace kept interrupting me while I was directing and tensions in the control room became so great that I ordered her to go back to her office. Such a challenge to her authority was until then unheard-of. Grace did return to her office, but never referred to the incident. However, the fact that the programme idea survived was entirely down to her. She was a fearsome fighter for the freedom of broadcasting and fortunately her qualities, rather than her faults, were acknowledged by the then Director General Sir Hugh Carleton Greene. She fought her way through the assistants and chief assistants to the DG's desk and explained what our intentions were. Hugh Greene was a great supporter of the BBC's drive to use broadcasting for the public good. He said he would defend such a programme against the critical voices of the manufacturing industry and their members of parliament, provided the programmes were good enough. The programmes were good enough. Grace relayed this to me with that firm, set look on her face which I came to know meant "If you let me down, you'll never work for me again."

"If you let me down, you'll never work for me again," is what Grace Wyndham Goldie's look said

Working for Grace was a two-sided coin. On one side she had probably more experience of broadcasting and certainly of factual television than anybody else of her generation, and she was willing to impart her experience to a young man just starting out in factual programming. The other side of the coin was the fact that she was under the constant strain of risk-taking, in an age when any new development in BBC Television was put under a microscope to look for its flaws. This strain began to show in her consumption of alcohol which made her, in some people's view, difficult to work with. It never worried me, but a lot of people felt damaged by her criticisms. One of my colleagues at the time told me that at a meeting we'd both attended with Grace, she had told me to get my hair cut. I had totally forgotten the incident, but he hadn't. However, Grace could become a liability as well as an asset to the BBC. Once, another colleague and friend had assiduously courted the Russian cultural attaché to be allowed into the USSR, which was very difficult to achieve at the time. He invited the attaché to hospitality, which in those days took place both before and after programme recordings. Grace was introduced to the attaché. She seized his copious lapels, hauled herself up on them, stared him in the eyes and said "We're free, are you?" Needless to say, the trip to the USSR had to wait some years before it took place.

For the trial series of six programmes of *Choice*, we showed the products more attractively. I was able to persuade Roy Laughton, who was running BBC Graphic Design, that this was a series that particularly needed excellent graphics for the product names and prices. He recommended a team that had made its reputation in the magazine world by doing the layout and graphics for a trendy publication called *Town*. I met Derek Birdsall, George Daulby, George Mayhew and Peter Wildbur, and they showed me exciting artwork, but I questioned if it would be successful on television. We requisitioned a studio that was out of use at the time, put cameras on their work and found that its style and quality did indeed come across very effectively. So they were hired and the series' appearance was vastly improved. One of the conditions that Carleton Greene had made was that the programme should be introduced by someone whom the audience could trust. Wyndham Goldie proposed Richard Dimbleby – the foremost broadcaster of his era. He could see that educating

Directors' style in the early 1970s

people in judging what was value for money and what was not, was a social benefit so he agreed to be presenter. The programme was shown in the early evening, when consumers would be most likely to see it. It never got a massive audience, but it was surprisingly successful because people found it useful. We paved the way for consumer programmes on BBC Television.

By now I was a fully fledged producer, working at the television studios in Lime Grove. I had started directing and producing, as was the custom in those days, wearing a suit and tie. By the time we got to the third series, the fashion for television producers had become more casual and we could wear open-necked shirts and display other signs of informality. By the time I left *Choice* and started to make documentaries, the media were entirely dressed in jeans. Men's hair had always been neatly

A junior television director was expected to dress like a business executive

cropped short. As well as clothes there came a media hairstyle: longish hair, but cut meticulously. I still go to the hairdresser, Trevor Daniel, who I found in Vidal Sassoon in 1968. Since then he has set up his own business near Berkeley Square and he's seen me through every hair variation for men ever since.

Working on *Choice* was to throw an interesting sidelight on the relationships that developed in broadcasting. My wife and I had fallen in love as a result of the shared nervous exhaustion involved in live broadcasting. I developed a relationship in a different dimension as a result of *Choice*. One of the researchers,

By the 1970s hairstyles had loosened up

Sue McConachy, had been to a girls' prep school, Dunottar, on the opposite side of Redhill Common from my school, Radnor House. One day when we were driving back from filming tests on, I think, saucepans, Sue pointed out we were passing a common which had been part of her youth. I was astonished because it was part of mine also. We stopped, got out for a walk and realised that we knew the same paths, clumps of bracken and so on. We discovered a further link: Sue, like me, was one-quarter German and, more astonishingly, had been born a few houses away from our house on the borders of Reigate and Redhill. It became a lifelong friendship.

CHAPTER EIGHT

Old photos tell new stories

Huw Wheldon had risen from being a presenter of children's programmes to a substantial on-screen figure, fronting as well as editing the BBC's foremost television arts programme *Monitor*. He was also responsible for what was to become the Documentary department. It was while I was on attachment to BBC Television Talks department in London at Lime Grove that I reaped the benefit of having saved him from destroying the matchstick model while on air all those years ago. He came across to me one day in the canteen and said "I've got some galley proofs of a book that I think you ought to look at and see if it could be turned into a documentary." I had always admired documentary makers since the days of the film club at school, when I had seen films like *Night Mail*, directed by Harry

Huw Weldon

Watt and Basil Wright, and *Housing Problems*, made by Arthur Elton. This had been the first film documentary where ordinary people spoke to camera in their own words. I wanted to use documentary techniques to make historical and other figures and situations come to life for the television audience.

At the time of Huw's proposal I was directing for a new live political programme called *Gallery*. I was surprised and, I suppose, flattered by this approach. I took the galley proofs home with me and read them. It was the story of a Victorian colonial governor based on the biography written by his grandson James Pope-Hennessy, who was a young writer of some fame, having won the Hawthornden Prize at the age of 21. I reported to Huw that it was certainly an interesting story and added that while doing the political show, I'd learned how to use still photographs to tell stories from a woman director who'd worked on film for the Central

Filming in a pharmacy for the political programme *Gallery*: **prescriptions, which had been free, now carried a charge – not a popular move**

Office of Information. Huw said "Well, why don't you take a short sequence and show me how you do that?" A researcher had told me that the Colonial Office was being merged with the Foreign Office and all its photographic archives were going to be thrown away. As someone who cared about photography, that pained me as I could see there would be valuable material there if we could intercept it between the Colonial Office and the rubbish tip. So the researcher Charles Denton (who later became a documentary maker and eventually ran an ITV company) and I found that in Victorian times governors chose aides-de-camp who had an ability with the new scientific art called 'photography'. They would get them to photograph the lands to be governed, before and after the governors' rule. There were therefore tons of pictures, including of most of the places where Sir John Pope-Hennessy had been appointed. Sir John had become a governorship appointee because he was an Irish MP in the British Parliament who had caused a certain amount of turmoil in various debates and deeply irritated Disraeli, the Prime Minister. Disraeli got the Colonial Secretary to post Pope-Hennessy to distant lands, whence he hoped he would not return. His first posting was to a particularly fever-riven island off what is now called Indonesia, Labuan.

Miraculously, Pope-Hennessy survived and so the Colonial Secretary, anxious this time to please Gladstone, posted him to what was known as 'the white man's grave' – Sierra Leone. By this time he'd married and had a son and, although the fever didn't affect Sir John, sadly it took his small child instead. There was then some sympathy for the Pope-Hennessys and he was sent to Hong Kong as governor. However he was not a very sociable man, seldom coming down from his hillside house to join in the social life of the English Hong Kong traders or merchants, known as 'taipans', and once again he found himself sent to a difficult post, this time as governor of Barbados. Pope-Hennessy sympathised with the slave workers and represented their grievances to the Colonial Office. The indigenous people were rising up against their white slave owners and it was said that this was the first and only time in British colonial history when "the natives had rebelled in the firm and correct belief that the Governor was on their side."

This attitude so displeased the Colonial Office that they moved him to Mauritius, where he withdrew even further from society. He ran the island from his isolated home by getting papers sent up to him, signing them and sending them back down. The Colonial Office was so concerned about this that

**James Pope-Hennessy
at his desk in Holland Park**

another governor was sent to investigate and eventually Pope-Hennessy was retired. He stood for Parliament again, went on the hustings in rain and cold – and died of pneumonia. This story, *Strange Excellency*, was told with stills, music and a good script which was the combined work of James Pope-Hennessy and me.

James was overtly homosexual, in those years before this was decriminalised by the Home Secretary Roy Jenkins. To a young man from the suburbs, even one who worked for the BBC, the people at James' parties were a revelation. The guests varied from aristocrats to guardsmen and many from the art world. These included a well-known art dealer, Kasmin, with a gallery in Bond Street. One of Kasmin's clients was a young man from Yorkshire, a student at the Royal College of Art, David Hockney. He was charming and, as I was told by James, talented, but his appearance was a bit of a shock: he was wearing green eye shadow and lipstick. James taught me a lot about what might now be known as the 'gay' scene. This included the fact that, within the Guards, going out with an

Silver prize for *Strange Excellency* **at the Berlin International competition**

older man was known as 'fitting'. This was because, if a rich older man picked up a young guardsman, he would take him first to the Turkish baths in Jermyn Street, where they would have a steamy time in a cubicle to themselves, and then on to the older man's tailor and outfitter for a tailored suit, hence the use of the word 'fitting'.

Strange Excellency did not just entertain the Tuesday documentary audience but, when entered for the international television competition in Berlin in 1964, it won a silver prize. As it turned out, it was beginner's luck or, more correctly, I had the good storytelling editorial guidance of Huw Wheldon to steer me.

You're only as good as your last programme

My second documentary was a wonderful story about a bibliographer, Thomas James Wise. He was such an authority on books that he was able to invent 'first editions' whose publication preceded those of the known first editions of people such as the poet Browning and other Victorian literary figures.

Wise was able to sell these effectively-forged 'first editions' at a premium price because, as the foremost bibliographer in London, it was thought there could be no higher recommendation than his. His fraud was uncovered by two young book men, John Carter and Graham Pollard. They were suspicious of this plethora of pre-first-edition 'first editions' and took examples to experts on typefaces and paper. They discovered that the serif on the letter 'j' in some of the 'pre-first editions' could not have been made with the metal in use on the date that Wise said they had been printed. Similarly the paper was found to contain a chemical that was not used in papermaking at the time. One of the contributors to the programme was Stanley Morison, head designer of The Monotype Corporation. He recognised my surname and asked "Was you father Frank Steltzer?" I said

A tribute to Max Steltzer in an American trade magazine from May 1933

"When he was born, yes. His name was changed at the beginning of the First World War, when German names could bring a brick through your window." Morison said "You realise your grandfather worked for me?" I'd known he worked for Monotype, but I hadn't known he was on the design team. Morison continued "You need to know that he was an enormously talented type designer and after German nationals were interned at the beginning of the war, I realised I needed him back on my team."

This was the first time I had understood how talented my grandfather really was, or had had any real insight into my father's family history. At this point I sent the camera crew for what they described afterwards as the longest coffee break they'd ever had. Morison then told me that he'd made the decision to get my grandfather Max Steltzer, who'd by this time changed his surname to Bonner, out of the internment camp. He had gone to the highest level relating to the government's use of the press, which later became the Ministry of Information. He told them that in order to get the very best visibility in the only medium that counted at that time – the press – he had to have my grandfather back at work. Max was duly freed and set to work on Morison's team again.

In return, I told Morison my father's story of a pre-war visit to England by his German cousin, Horst, before the tensions between Britain and Germany made such a trip impossible. My father had taken him to the Last Night of the Proms, where Horst found himself obliged to sing *Rule Britannia*.

There was, however, a sad postscript to my grandfather's story: the strain of internment had been too much for my grandmother, who had escaped the massacre in Armenia only a few years earlier. Her mental health suffered from that experience – and I like to think that she also missed having her only son, my father, with her when he had been sent to Dollar Academy in Scotland at the beginning of the war.

The Wise Forgeries was a terrific story but, without the experienced Huw Wheldon looking over my shoulder, I failed to tell it properly. I began to think my only future might be to return to live studio directing in Current Affairs. My morale was at an all-time low and I feared my fledgling documentary-making career was at an end.

But just at that time a remarkable man, Francis Chichester, was sailing a boat single-handed around the world, including going round Cape Horn. Michael Peacock, the Controller of BBC2, commissioned me to make a 30-minute documentary on Chichester's life. I went to see Chichester's wife, the formidable Sheila, and she

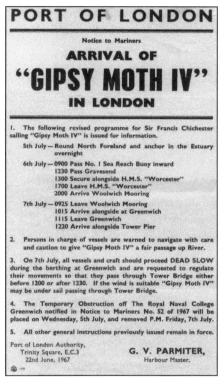

Port of London Authority schedule, showing Chichester's arrival at Greenwich, where he was knighted

told me that Francis had attempted to fly round the world in a de Havilland Gipsy Moth in the 1930s. Not only did he have amazing adventures, including having to rebuild his plane on an island in the middle of the Tasman Sea, but she also let on that in the loft of their house in St James's were his photographs of that trip. For me, who knew how to use still photographs in story-telling, this was a treasure trove. She of course said I could not take them out of the house, but I was able to get a photographer in to copy them. I then filmed them with a rostrum camera and we used some newsreel footage of Francis in the latterday *Gipsy Moth IV* yacht. We also had some interviews with his friends and solo yachtsmen rivals such as 'Blondie' Hasler. The old man made it round Cape Horn and sailed up the South Atlantic and into Plymouth Sound on 28th May 1967. Huge crowds assembled on Plymouth Hoe to greet him and my film, *The World His Challenge*, was put out on the eve of his arrival, to some acclaim. Later BBC1's Children's Programmes showed the film and then, when Francis Chichester was knighted by the Queen at Greenwich, it was shown again. My documentary-making career was reprieved.

CHAPTER NINE

Documentary lift-off

The success of *The World His Challenge* caught the attention of Aubrey Singer, who was the head of the whole three departments of BBC Features group and who had a passion for innovation. He had accepted a programme proposal from the Travel and Adventure Unit in one of the Features departments to make a film about Britain from the air. Despite the limitations to what could be done from the air at the time, the film had been a success. As a result Singer contracted British Executive Air Services to provide a generous allocation of flying hours. He chose a producer, Eddie Mirzoeff, who had been part of my team while we were still at Lime Grove, and challenged him to find a

Eddie Mirzoeff (left) and Ian Stone, cameraman, on an early flight along the North Devon coast

Directors and cameramen during training, discovering how low they could fly – providing they got the correct permission

use for the helicopter flying time. Eddie came up with the idea of *Bird's Eye View of Britain*, looking at various aspects of Britain from the air.

One of the first things Eddie organised was a tutorial session from Albert Lamorisse, a French director, best known for his film *The Red Balloon*, but who had made several films using helicopters. Lamorisse taught us things that we needed to know. "Helicopter shots," he said "are all middle and you have to invent a beginning and an end for them." For example, if you want to film a train, you can film alongside it but then you have to turn across the front of it so that the film editor has a point to cut to the next shot. Lamorisse also led us to understand that this didn't just apply to moving objects but to how you can reveal whole new scenes with a helicopter. Eddie was later to devise what I called 'the Mirzoeff mountain reveal', which was to fly up a mountain cliff face that would fill the screen before suddenly revealing the landscape or cityscape below. Meanwhile I invented 'the Bonner cloud reveal': on a day when there were nice white puffy clouds in the sky we would fly the helicopter into the top of a cloud, disconnect the engine from the rotor (this was called autorotation) and let the helicopter drop through the remainder of the cloud to reveal the landscape below. This was not a dangerous manoeuvre but, as well as learning about the grammar of filming from a helicopter, we also needed to find out what the helicopter could and could not do. One manoeuvre which I attempted involved a 'downwind turn' where the tail rotor no longer has any leverage into the wind, in order to get 360 degree coverage of a monument. I had to settle for 240 degrees, when my pilot Peter Pekowski warned me off. He came up with the saying that I was to remember at a later date. "There are old helicopter pilots and there are bold helicopter pilots, but as far as I know, there are no old, bold helicopter pilots." All this education in aerial filming was achieved over two days in the projection room with Albert Lamorisse and a day at the airport at Kidlington with our two pilots, Ted Novak and Peter Pekowski.

Eddie himself made several wonderful films in the series, one of them showing the great British tradition of seaside holidays, with a script by the later-to-become poet laureate, John Betjeman. This was very successful and generated another Betjeman collaboration, *Metro-Land*, for a different series, showing the development of London suburbia to the north-west along the extension of the Metropolitan railway. There were more flying hours yet to be used so another producer, Tim Slessor, boldly filmed the length of Britain and entitled it *From Bishop Rock to Muckle Flugga*. I was one of the other producers asked to find a use for the helicopter hours and I came up with two ideas. One was about the history of transport and what it had done to the face of Britain, with a script by the historian Correlli Barnett. The other was a film of my own devising, with a script by John Lloyd, about leisure in Britain, which we called *The British Way of Fun and Games*.

The moment before all was revealed

The latter film had a number of difficulties in its making. I'd observed that the advertising industry was portraying ever more glamorous impressions of Britain at play. As a parody, I devised a sequence whereby a beautiful young woman would drive a Lotus sports car along an empty beach, pull up beside the sea and dive in. It was supposed to be apparent that as she got out of the car she was, as was the fashion in advertising at the time, unclothed. This was to be shot on the emptiest beach we could find, Pendine Sands in south Wales, using a model who agreed to appear without clothes. When she arrived, the night before the filming, I greeted her and told her roughly what was expected of her. I failed to ask to see her naked – a fatal mistake, as it turned out. The next morning the beautiful Lotus sports car and the beautiful girl were married up and I took off in the helicopter with Geoff Mulligan, the cameraman. We found precisely the height and angle that would catch her pulling up, getting out of the car and running into the sea. It wasn't going to be possible to do more than one take because the car tire marks were going to ruin the pristine stretch of sand. I gave the order for the car to start moving and the helicopter followed. The ground crew signalled for the car to pull up at an agreed point. As the model got out and ran to the sea it became apparent, even from the air, that she appeared not to be naked. It turned out she had been to the Mediterranean on a previous shoot and the bikini marks from her sunbathing made it look from the air as if she was wearing a white bikini. So the sequence, as I had it in mind, was a failure.

Briefs, in a totally different context, were to feature again before the day was out. Our researcher, Christine Whittaker, had arranged for us, at the end of a hot day, to be given entry to the Port Talbot Steelworks staff swimming pool. The changing-room for men was totally communal – and huge, like an aircraft hangar. Desperate to get into the water I threw off my clothes and, as I took off my trousers, I heard what seemed to be a communal gasp from around me. I had forgotten that, for comfort, I was in the habit of wearing Marks & Spencer women's briefs, which offered much better support than the men's pants of the time! Worse still, they had been in the wash with some red garment which had run and stained them pink. Effectively, many dozens of steelworkers were transfixed to see every stereotype of a media man fulfilled!

Another sequence in *The British Way of Fun and Games* was to follow a lone climber up to the peak of the Brecon Beacons, then swing the helicopter round and pan up to see that marvellous wild landscape. When we got to the peak we discovered there were two people enjoying a picnic underneath it, who would spoil the shot we'd planned. I couldn't do without that sequence in the film, so there was nothing for it but to get the pilot to hover while I lowered myself out of the helicopter to ask the

Approaching a Brecon Beacons peak from the air

picknickers to move round to the other side of the peak so that they would not be in shot. They were two middle aged ladies, who were none too pleased to have their scenic lunch, which they'd expended enormous amounts of energy to achieve, so rudely interrupted. They turned out to be skilled negotiators and, seeing that the helicopter was burning fuel and that I needed to get back into it fast, they demanded a fee for moving round the Beacon and hiding from the camera. I eventually agreed to pay them £100, but had absolutely no cash on me at all. I scrambled back into the helicopter with difficulty and asked the cameraman or the pilot to lend me money. Geoff fortunately had his expenses with him and was able to lend me the cash. I then had to dismount from the helicopter, hand over the money and get back in again. Not only was this an exhausting and slightly frightening process, but we had probably burned a lot more than £100's worth of fuel in order to allow me to do the negotiation, get the money and film the sequence.

For every difficulty in making that film, there were some moments of great joy. Travelling north from London we flew

The Pontcysyllte Aqueduct carries the Llangollen Canal over the River Dee

over Wenlock Edge at seven in the morning, as mist was coming up that wonderful cliff face. What joy it would have been for A E Housman to be with us. Our target was the Pontcysyllte Aqueduct that carried the Llangollen Canal over the River Dee valley. I planned the shot to move from a little waterfall on the River Dee up one of the pillars of the aqueduct, arriving at the top perfectly timed with a barge entering the shot from the right hand side. Once again there was no possibility of a retake and I and the whole crew were very relieved when it worked.

The commentary for *The British Way of Fun and Games*
was read by June Whitfield, Garfield Morgan and John le Mesurier

The final sequence of *The British Way of Fun and Games* consisted of the lights being turned on at Southend-on-Sea. It meant that we had to film at dusk and afterwards return the helicopter to London, with Peter the pilot planning to leave it overnight at Battersea Heliport. Peter navigated using the Thames for direction as it curved between Essex and Kent, with the sunset reflected on its surface. I heard him call the control tower at Battersea "Battersea Heliport, this is helicopter Golf Alpha Whisky

Foxtrot Lima requesting approach to land and overnight." There was a pause and a voice came back "Helicopter Golf Alpha Whisky Foxtrot Lima, we are closed." Peter responded with "What do you suggest?" There was a longer pause and Control came back with "You must contact London Airport approach and see whether you can land on the north side of Heathrow." Peter duly called up London Airport, which was busy guiding in 'Speedbirds' (which is what BOAC – now British Airways – used to use as a call sign), along with Pan Am and all the other international carriers. Eventually a voice came back over the air "Helicopter Golf Alpha Whisky Foxtrot Lima, fly up the A4 and turn left at the slip road." Peter turned to Geoff and me, saying "Which slip road does he mean?" Geoff said "You can borrow my AA book if you like, Peter." Eventually we turned left down the correct slip road and landed just to the north of runway two-eight right (the northern runway at that time).

Sadly, soon after we finished our series we heard that our helicopter mentor, Albert Lamorisse, had been killed in a helicopter crash in what was then Persia. He had been making a documentary for the Shah based on a medieval story of the four winds and, at the Shah's request, had gone back to add some extra shots of modern Persia. Ironically it was the wind that, curling over the dam that he was filming, swept his aircraft into its face, killing all on board. We were very fortunate to have had access to his helicopter filming experience so soon before he died.

The *Bird's Eye View* series, which was made by several different directors, was judged to be a success. It was enjoyable and educational viewing. I therefore proposed that we should do a European series, one in each of the major countries of the continent. For the pilot episode I wanted to shoot in Switzerland, partly because I'd previously filmed amongst the mountains there, but primarily because every frame of film you shot in that landscape could be a thing of beauty. I felt that an experimental programme shot in Switzerland would act as a sales stimulus for the whole *Bird's Eye View of Europe* idea.

I arranged with the helicopter company to have the same Alouette and pilot Peter Pekowski that I'd used in Britain, to fly out to Switzerland. Meanwhile my researcher hired a twin-engined Cessna light aircraft so that we could together note down the settings which we should weave into the film. We managed to complete that reconnaissance in half a day, but the film's shooting was to take 21 days and it was likely that a whole series would prove to be rather too expensive for the BBC at that time. However the programme, a co-production with Swiss Television, was to prove difficult in matters other than sheer expense. This was as a result of the complex history of the country, involving the 'Eidgenossen': the sworn cantons of the Federation. The original 13 cantons had grown by now to 25, each with a different government and several of them with different languages. But there was also a sort of resentment that a foreign broadcaster was coming in and shooting a film that Swiss Television should have thought of for itself. So we had layers of political difficulty: tensions with the Swiss broadcasters, tensions with the cantonal governments and even trouble with the mayors of particular cities. An example of the latter was with Zermatt, a beautiful ski resort and spa in the shadow of Mont Blanc. The mayor of Zermatt was (almost unbelievably) called Constant Cashin. He owned his own helicopter company and was anxious that we pay him to use his aircraft on the grounds that "my pilot knows every inch of these mountains." I was determined not to have all of Peter Pekowski's hours of filming sidelined for a mayor's pride and bank balance. But how to overcome Herr Cashin's obduracy? Fortunately Peter had developed a close working relationship with the official at the Luftampt – the Swiss Air Ministry – with whom we had to negotiate all our flying permissions. It appeared that they'd both flown multi-engine aircraft before moving to helicopters. When Peter told his Luftampt friend about Herr Cashin's machinations, the official sided with us and telephoned the mayor to tell him so. Herr Cashin never spoke to us again, but we managed to get our footage of the town, the railway and the surrounding mountains, which is what we wanted. The BBC was not prepared to take *Bird's Eye View of Europe* further than Switzerland, but the Swiss were extremely happy to use their rights under the co-production agreement to show the film for as many times as they wanted. In fact for many years Swiss Television showed *Bird's Eye View of Switzerland* every Swiss National Day, 1st August, which made me feel that all the effort had been worthwhile.

Surprisingly, perhaps, Swiss Television had come to value my judgement and I was later made chairman of the pre-selection jury for the Golden Rose of Montreux Festival, well known at the time as the premier award for comedy programmes.

CHAPTER TEN

The journey into documentaries

It's a source of wonder to me, let alone to friends and colleagues, that I came to make 28 documentaries in ten years for the BBC. How can I, as a suburban nonentity, account for this? The answer, and it maybe gives some guidance to others, is that I had a mix of talents – none of them outstanding – but, in combination, the correct formula: I had inherited a graphic sense from my grandfather, the German type designer; I had learned storytelling from my mother and the many books that she and I had read together; and a restless inquisitive element in my character meant that I always wanted to find out the story behind the story. But above all I had the one thing I and anybody else in many careers, let alone broadcasting, needed, which was luck – the most important of which was the luck of a training in the Army. This taught me leadership and a basic ability to overcome difficulties, as well as developing a certain sort of courage – if you're a producer in broadcasting, you're always going to have as many difficulties as you can cope with. So when my lodger in Bristol, the fellow BBC producer Christopher Ralling and I agreed that he would teach me how to make film and I would teach him how to make live television, it was the beginning. He'd actually got into the BBC on the basis of a 16mm film he'd made when he was in Australia. I had no such experience to offer. In fact, Chris was a talented filmmaker but he never really took to live television. I was a good live director, but only slowly began to absorb the lessons of how to tell stories on film, from better film makers than me. Chris went on to make some of the early 'drama documentaries' which are still remembered for their excellence – *The Fight Against Slavery*, *The Search for the Nile* and *The Voyage of Charles Darwin*.

Chris Ralling's talents led to his being recruited by the then primary current affairs programme in London, *Panorama*, which was made up of three or four short film items in each hour-long edition. Soon I realised that to progress, I would have also to move to London and I had the contact with Grace Wyndham Goldie as a possible pathway. Surprisingly she telephoned to tell me to look out for one of the BBC's internal job advertisements. It was for an attachment – a brief period of work – in London to her department, Television Talks. In the BBC you were seldom parachuted into jobs; there was always a competitive board interview, but some were more competitive than others. When I turned up Grace was on the board and asked the sort of questions that she knew I could answer. So I got my attachment, which turned out to be a crucial part of my television education.

Broadcasters at that time were prevented from covering certain political subjects by something called 'the 14-day rule'. This rule, laid down by Parliament itself, involved not covering what Parliament was actually going to discuss in the next fortnight. Of course some of the more important debates were last-minute affairs, so reporting on them was well-nigh impossible. At that time cameras were not allowed in the House. We had no knowledge necessarily of the more important debates that were coming up and any analysis had to be studio based and retrospective, requiring MPs to be brought down from Westminster to Shepherd's Bush. This meant that coverage of parliamentary affairs was going to have its limitations. However, at the time the Director General was Hugh Carleton Greene, who had fought against censorship for all his journalistic career. When Leonard Miall, who was the actual head of Television Talks (Grace Wyndham Goldie was his deputy), put the idea of a weekly programme covering current political issues up the BBC command chain, it was such a controversial matter that it reached Carleton Greene's desk. The message came back down that a trial series should be agreed and the DG would take responsibility if complaints were raised in the House of Commons. The series was named *Gallery*.

I was one of two junior producers on the *Gallery* team. The other was a graduate trainee called Anthony Smith (later in life he was to be President of Magdalen College, Oxford). The team was led by a man called John Grist and his second in command was Jack Ashley (who later became a Labour MP). Political responsibility for the show fell on John and Jack. John crumpled under the pressure and gave way to flu, Jack mysteriously got snowed-in in his home town of Widnes, and the future of this crucial series was left in the hands of

The 1959 Labour Party political broadcast was introduced by Anthony Wedgwood Benn

these two neophytes, a young trainee director from Bristol and the graduate trainee just down from Oxford. I had the greater television experience and it was my view that we'd better do something that people would want to watch and if possible talk about afterwards. Fortunately a book about the 1959 general election, by Joseph Trenaman and Denis McQuail, had just been published and the party election broadcasts had been rather more adventurous than usual, so we could show extracts from

them and then hold a discussion. For this we cast Tony
Wedgwood Benn for Labour, Jeremy Thorpe for the Liberals
and Geoffrey Johnson Smith for the Conservatives. It was
chaired by a fluent Canadian academic called Bob McKenzie,
a professor of politics and sociology.

Meanwhile there had been an incident in South Africa, the
Sharpeville massacre, in which the South African police had
mown down demonstrating black residents. Tony Smith realised
that this would have implications for Britain where there were
strong feelings voiced in Parliament about apartheid, the
Afrikaner strategy for separating blacks and whites. He ordered
some newsreel of the Sharpeville massacre, which was fairly
shocking, and got an eminent journalist to provide a commentary
to the film. You could always tell whether a programme had
been a success or not by the way people greeted you in the
Lime Grove canteen at coffee time the following day. When
Tony and I arrived for our coffee, people met us in the eyes
and one or two even said "Well done." Miraculously John Grist
recovered from flu, the snows in Widnes melted and Jack Ashley
returned. Although there were political items on the current
affairs programmes *Panorama*, *Tonight* and *This Week*, the great
burden of coverage of subjects of interest to those concerned
with politics was done by *Gallery*. The programme, under a
different team though with John Grist still as editor, ran for
several years, by which time politics was the stuff of many
different television programmes. A key result of the trial series
of *Gallery* was Parliament's abandoning of the 14-day rule.

The reportage documentaries

Soon afterwards, in 1967, the old Talks department was split
into Current Affairs, Music & Arts and General Features. I got
placed in General Features, which had a wonderful head of

department, Antony Jay, later famous for being a co-writer of *Yes, Minister*. Alas he correctly saw the head of General Features as an extremely boring role and he became part of the first independent production group, JBM Productions, made up of producers of the popular Talks programme, *Tonight*. As well as Jay there was the ex-editor of *Tonight*, Donald Baverstock, and his deputy Alasdair Milne. There was a struggle to replace Antony Jay because nobody wanted the job. I would have quite liked it but, aged 26, was considered too young and so another of the *Tonight* refugees, Gordon Watkins, was given the job. Though he was a good script editor he was considered a very poor head of department. Worse still, General Features was moved out of Lime Grove to a building above Ealing Broadway station, Villiers House. The telephones didn't work, none of the windows opened and it had appallingly bad air conditioning. When we all complained, the administrative man in the team called Arthur Radley, came up with the famous dictum "If you throw the telephones that don't work through the windows that don't open, at least you'll feel better!"

"If you throw the telephones that don't work through the windows that don't open, at least you'll feel better!"

The executive who ruled the Features group, Aubrey Singer, had a substantial background in the media. He had started in the business as a film editor with the Shell Film Unit, but later joined BBC Outside Broadcasts. When I said I wanted to go on making documentaries, having just finished my Francis Chichester film, Singer told me that he'd got on contract Christopher Brasher, the famous athlete and one-time reporter on the *Tonight* programme, and that he had two programmes of his contract yet to be made. Did I have any ideas? I was keen to explore the possibility of making a film about an American mid-air collision which had dumped four H-bombs in Spanish territory in 1966. Singer wisely pointed out that, though Brasher was a good journalist, his enthusiasm and skill were in relation to athletics and mountain climbing. We reached a deal whereby if I made a film that Chris Brasher wanted to do about climbing the North Face of the Eiger, I would be allowed to make a film with him, on a subject that interested me, about the US Air Force mid-air collision. Three H-bombs had fallen into the sea and one of them landed on the village of Palomares, which had changed little since the 13th century.

Plutonium had been scattered in the sandy soil to the south of the village when the bomb hit the ground, and the villagers were alarmed by the clicking radiation meters that the US Air Force had planted around the village to measure the radiation that was being given off. There was no chance of the bomb exploding; safety measures meant that there couldn't be even a conventional explosion, let alone a nuclear one. The US Air Force had sent bulldozers to clear up the plutonium but nobody, neither the US Air Force nor the Spanish government, had explained to the villagers that there was no threat to them. However an aristocrat, the Duchess of Medina Sidonia, who had survived Franco's fascist republican takeover, decided to adopt the village, as it was on land that had been owned by her family since the time of the Spanish Armada. She took it upon herself to educate the villagers and I arrived with my film crew just after this process had started. We were able to film her describing to everyone what had happened and how the village was not threatened by the accident in the way that they had come to believe. Long after we left, she continued her battle for the villagers, to the point where she was eventually imprisoned.

The Duchess took it upon herself to educate the worried villagers

My first trip to America

One of the benefits of making that film was it took me to America for the first time. Neither Brasher nor I knew enough at that point about nuclear physics to say whether there was any threat to people's health in the longer term. We had to go to Washington to get some film of the other bombs that had fallen into the Mediterranean. We decided that, while there, we would fix to go and see the nuclear physicists at Los Alamos in New Mexico, who were at that time the world's experts on the threat posed by any nuclear accident. Los Alamos was a strange village, set up as the headquarters for the original experiments with nuclear explosions in the Arizona desert. As happened often in America in those days, we were given a great welcome as representatives of the BBC. Top scientists willingly explained nuclear radiation and its strengths and limitations to us. Los Alamos was like a university faculty in the middle of the desert: highly intelligent people all pursuing the development of the 20th century's deadliest invention. As with any university, they had the money to organise their entertainment. When we came down to breakfast in the guest house at Los Alamos, we found Julian Bream tuning his guitar and grumbling at what the high temperatures and altitude were doing to his instrument. We discovered that the Duchess was not in any sense wrong about the fact there was no danger to the villagers, once the plutonium had been removed.

Meanwhile I had to try to persuade the American Navy to let us have under-sea film footage of the unexploded bombs that had fallen into the Mediterranean. I went to the Pentagon, expecting to be rebuffed, only to be invited in to the film library, where an assistant was waiting to produce such film as I had requested. Doubtless if there had been anything really secret I would not have been allowed access, but they were

New York from the top of the Empire State building

perfectly willing to let me see — and subsequently transmit — some of the footage from the American submersible which had found the H-bombs intact. It was one of the joys of filming in America that I was to discover that, where authorities in Britain would say "No" the Americans, to my amazement, said "Yes." American commerce and industry at that time also took positive positions on many other matters. For instance, I had the wonderful experience of flying in a helicopter from the top of the Pan Am building in Park Avenue. I was led through a nightclub on the 56th floor onto the roof and scrambled aboard a giant helicopter. To take off at night, climbing round the brightly lit art-deco tower of the Chrysler building and across the river to John F Kennedy airport, was an amazing experience. This represented, to me, the epitome of America at that time and its persistent drive to move ahead. In fact, frequently they went too far. Some years later, one of the helicopters landing on the Pan Am rooftop helipad toppled sideways and five people lost their lives. The service was closed down immediately.

Before we left Spain, the Duchess organised a party in her Madrid apartment for the film crew, Chris and me. This generous gesture was nearly compromised by our extremely handsome young assistant cameraman flirting with the Duchess' secretary, Mary Vee, who seemed to be responding to him. I sensed that the Duchess was upset by this behaviour and it took me no more than a minute or two to realise that the secretary was also the Duchess' lover. I signalled to Chris Brasher that we'd got to disentangle the amorous assistant cameraman from an embarrassing situation that might have put paid to any further help from the Duchess. The young assistant didn't know what he'd done wrong as Chris and I took an elbow each, marched him down the stairs and threw him in a taxi to take him back to the hotel.

As an account of an extraordinary nuclear event, *The Bombs of Palomares* made a good film. Unfortunately, before it was scheduled for transmission, the US Air Force lost another B-52 bomber over Greenland, scattering more plutonium in the snowy wastes there. There was no human habitation in that area, but the resulting news headlines meant that Paul Fox, then the Controller of BBC1, wanted to bring forward the transmission of *The Bombs of Palomares*. This meant it didn't have a proper billing in *Radio Times* – or the publicity that it deserved – and so, ironically *'Bombs'*, the more important of the pair of films I was making with Chris Brasher, received little coverage. On the other hand, *Climb up to Hell*, an account of the early attempts to climb the North Face of the Eiger, was a critical and audience success.

Chris Brasher's knowledge had been invaluable during the filming of the latter programme. I had always been fascinated by the attraction of mountain climbing ever since Chris Ralling, my good friend in Bristol, had told me a lot about the group of climbers for which Britain was famous, all of whom Brasher knew personally. One of those was Chris Bonington, who had climbed the North Face of the Eiger wearing as his protective

Setting up to film the great North Face of the Eiger.
Opposite: **One of our team of climbers, recreating the formidable task undertaken by climbers of the North Face**

clothing only his ex-Army *"British Warm, green, Officers for the wearing of"* (an overcoat). Brasher had seen that there was a film in the stories of these great climbers, starting with a former member of the Nazi Party, Heinrich Harrer, who later became famous for his book *Seven Years in Tibet*.

I had thought that if we got Harrer and all the later people who'd attempted the North Face, we'd have a dramatic story. Chris had agreed and used his various friends, including the cameraman John Clare, the famous climber Dougal Haston and Chris Bonington himself, to tell their stories. There was also the sad story of an American called John Harlin, who had fallen off the final icefield to his death. His film of the climb was retrieved and I negotiated with his widow for the rights to use it in the programme. It was incredibly dramatic, since he'd been holding the camera as he fell. With the help of music from Strauss' *Alpine Symphony*, I was able to put together a poignant evocation of the tragic side of climbing, which caught something of the hard magic of the North Face of the Eiger.

The film broke new ground by having all the accounts of the climbs told by the surviving climbers themselves. The result, with the Strauss music, was so emotive that Barbara Leigh-Hunt, the actress who I'd asked to read from Harlin's diary, told me that

the front of her blouse was wet with tears. Chris Brasher was able to delve into his knowledge to provide a more detailed than usual script for the film. He insisted on delivering his own commentary and, though he was an excellent writer, he had a voice like a corncrake. Although it detracted from the full impact of the film, it was at least clear and in some ways dramatic. *Climb up to Hell* was yet another step on the road to documentary achievement, which was to include the *Bird's Eye View* films, *In Search*

Jeni

of the Real Che Guevara and *Coronet for a Prince*. This was to keep me going on the basis of three films a year.

I could not have done so without the courageous support of my wife Jeni, who brought up our three children through the difficult years of their adolescence and was really responsible for helping them grow into creative and successful adulthood.

I could not have achieved so much without the courageous support of my wife Jeni

The birth of *Coronet for a Prince* was unusual in that it was a co-production between BBC Outside Broadcasts and the Goldsmiths' Company of the City of London. It was about the making of the crown for Prince Charles' investiture at Caernarfon in 1969. This was a lovely little film to have been asked to make, collaborating with the designer and maker of the coronet, Louis Osman. He had persuaded the Goldsmiths' Company to let him use an Elizabethan house in Northamptonshire, Canons Ashby, where with two apprentices he designed and built the crown. It was an ideal location for this film. However, the process was not

Louis Osman working on the crown

without incident: while we were filming, a crack appeared in the crown. Osman had to remake that section and we had to reshoot the sequence that had shown it being made.

On completion, the film was given a private screening for the Prince at the Goldsmiths' Company. The warden of the Company came across the room in his tricorn hat and introduced me to Prince Charles. Clearly the Goldsmiths' Company had leaked the story to the Palace, because the first thing Prince Charles said to me was "So you're the person who broke the crown." The film was shown on television as part of the introduction to the outside broadcast coverage of the investiture at Caernarfon.

CHAPTER ELEVEN

The Kensington House mob

The unusual nature of the General Features department, in that it had no specialisms but could produce entirely new sorts of programmes, meant that the young producers and assistants had a freedom at that time that was available nowhere else in the BBC Television service. They were a bright young group of programme-makers, who were in a sense misfits for any other department. They readily joined in a campaign to get us moved back from Ealing to the relative civilisation of Shepherd's Bush. We succeeded and got put in an office block, Kensington House. This was built to follow the curve of a disused railway siding and though its architecture may have left a lot to be desired, the departments posted there, which included Sport, Music & Arts and General Features, were a happy if somewhat rebellious bunch. This little department could have become a dustbin into which were thrown programme ideas that didn't fit in the 'classical' departments of Drama, Current Affairs, Documentary etc. In fact, this represented an enormous benefit, both to the producers of General Features and of the BBC's range of programmes. We were able to try wholly new formats and styles, and it's not hubris to say that we were part of moving the BBC Television service out of the styles of the fifties into the greater risk-taking for which the BBC became admired during the sixties and beyond.

Kensington House, like all BBC buildings in those days, had a bar and various of the departments would retire there for

The executives in Television Centre regarded 'the Kensington House mob' as a danger to the corporate structure of the BBC

drinks at the end of the day and compare their grievances against the BBC hierarchy. The executives in Television Centre regarded 'the Kensington House mob', as they called us, as a danger to the corporate structure of the BBC. I and many others were very happy to be tarred with that brush and various documents making proposals to improve BBC Television were passed upwards from Ken House, as it became known, to the hierarchy. One of these papers was known as 'The SIMPU Paper'. The initials stood for Small Independent Multi-Purpose Units. This arose from the fact that all of we documentary directors had an ideal crew in mind to work with on our films. I believed that if units could be set up that were self-contained, we'd get a higher quality of film-making. This ran counter not just to the programming side of the BBC but also the Facilities people, who were strongly against it because it didn't allow them to schedule their camera and sound men as freely as they wanted to. So SIMPU was blocked at a fairly high level. However it had an afterlife in the sort of units that independent producers subsequently set up, to produce work for Channel Four. Many of those units were led by producers who had worked in Ken House or Bristol, or other places where production and creative technical staff had benefited from the experience of working together over a period of time.

A programme experiment

The peak of both revolutionary and experimental television was reached with a series proposed by four General Features producers:

Jonathan Stedall, Richard Taylor, Lawrence Gordon Clark and myself, whose revolutionary nature led to us being christened 'The Gang of Four' (a reference to the four Chinese revolutionary leaders). Looking back, the series we produced, *What Sort of a World do We Want?*, was grossly self-indulgent but it actually had the distinctive quality which infused many of the General Features programmes. Stedall, who was a Montessori education man, made a fascinating programme about it, at a time when that style of schooling had not yet become popular. Richard Taylor made a programme about industrial trade unions which advocated union members being invited onto management boards. Lawrence Gordon Clark was into art and architecture and produced a fascinating film showing that art could brighten the buildings with which we surrounded ourselves.

I made a programme about the future of the family, at a time when there was a lot of criticism that the so-called 'nuclear family' (two parents and two or three children) was a limiting factor in social growth. The Scandinavians, I discovered, were much more advanced in matters of family, and I arranged to go to Denmark to film in a commune. Under an exchange scheme with Danmarks Radio, I had a Danish researcher, who found an ideal commune of some 50 people in a large house in the country. I filmed their daily life, including their Esalen psychological sessions, one Californian version of 'encounter groups'. Basically they were young middle class people – artists, musicians, architects and so on – and fairly well off. In one way they enjoyed living together but in another way, as one of them said to me "It is very difficult to love everybody." The tension between members of the group indicated by that statement was alleviated in some cases by the use of cannabis though, while I was there, none of the hard drugs were used. As an unsuspecting

"It is very difficult to love everybody," said one member of the commune incomer, I did not associate the fudge that I was offered with my coffee, with drugs. It turned out to be 'hash fudge' and because I was tempted by its deliciousness, it led me to having the only out-of-body experience of my life. The Esalen encounter group technique involved a session after dinner when everyone lay face up on the floor in a circle, with their feet at the hub. I was invited to join in. We all had to think of who we would like to make love to and silently visualise it.

The shower scene symbolised communal life – and steam obscured the nudity

This was a bit of a shock to a BBC innocent, added to which, in the midst of it all I found myself on the ceiling of the room looking down at all of us, including myself, in the circle. Between me and me, as it were, was an apparent oscilloscope trace of the music that was playing on the hi-fi – music by Country Joe McDonald and the Fish, a politically active San Francisco band of the time. The event was vivid and exciting, and quite outside my experience. The difficulty was to translate that into film without crossing the boundaries of taste required by public service broadcasting at the time and, despite my great care, the film was to get the BBC and me into trouble. I had woken the following morning feeling a bit bleary, but the film had to go on. I found a tasteful sequence in which one of the men went into the shower and had his back scrubbed by one of the women, who then had her back scrubbed by another man, and so on. The shower scene symbolised the nature of communal life and thenudity was helpfully obscured by steam.

Making this film also demonstrated the complexity of achieving that BBC shibboleth, 'balance'. There were no written rules, but we were all brought up within the Corporation to understand that balance between the factors involved in any programme was of paramount importance. The audience had to be given a clear insight into the elements that the average person might see as for or against any argument or situation. This weighing-up had to be translated to the audience's mind and as a producer one's responsibility was to give them the wherewithal to weigh one aspect of a situation or argument against its counterpart.

In this instance, the balance had to be between the case for the nuclear family of father, mother and children, and the case for communal living, with several families and individuals having a life together and making communal decisions. This wasn't easy to achieve, as there was no straightforward equivalence as in, say, political programmes of left versus right. Many would argue that it was simply right against wrong. In the end I found a method of balance in this complicated weighing-up: it lay in two sequences in the film. These were the communal shower sequence, against the interview on the sound track with the woman who had said "It is difficult to love everybody." It was not an exact balance, but it was the best I could do and it did give both arguments in a way that allowed the audience to reach their own conclusion.

CHAPTER TWELVE

Salvaging a series

A General Features series called *Explorers* was set up under the producer Michael Latham. He had chosen to direct the first film himself which was about Pizarro, the Spanish discoverer of the great wealth of the Aztecs and, ultimately, their conquerer. The shoot ran into formidable difficulties filming what in effect was period drama in the jungles and mountains of South America. Michael had to spend a large proportion of the series' budget to get the first film made at all. The deputy managing director of Television at the time, Robin Scott, was approached to provide a solution to get the remainder of the series made. He didn't have huge amounts of money in his budget. Experienced directors and producers such as David Cobham, Lawrence Gordon Clark, Fred Burnley and me were called together as a rescue party. Lawrence took on the directing of the film on Columbus, Fred the explorer Stanley, and David the Norwegian victor of the race to the South Pole, Roald Amundsen. I had the overall responsibility for the production of all three programmes, on a minimal budget. *Stanley* ran into trouble immediately, filming in the volatile political situation at the time in Zaire (now the Democratic Republic of the Congo), and we had to get out of the country fast.

Michael Latham, who was still associated with the series, proposed that we shoot it in Sierra Leone, since that ex-British

The politics of Zaire required permissions, which were not always forthcoming

colony was certainly friendlier than Zaire. We agreed to go there despite the entirely different landscape. Somehow Fred Burnley found locations that could pass as the jungles of central Africa and we were able to film. The story had scenes of battles with the locals and nobody in Sierra Leone had ever shot a bow and arrow, so we had to teach them to do so. Meanwhile our special effects people were setting up effects where bullets would apparently hit trees, behind which people were standing. Fred asked the cameraman to get close-ups of the shells hitting the trunks, with the locals out of focus behind the trees. In essence, the camera was closer to the explosions than the acting tribes people. When the first explosion blew tree pulp all over the camera lens, the cameraman flew into a rage, saying that it was dangerous and he was "walking off the set." As usual, I as the producer was turned to for a solution. It seemed to me that the cameraman would have to walk a very long way if he was going to get back to civilisation, so we waited. Sure enough, before long he returned without comment and we went on to the next shot – but this time with the camera further back from the explosions.

The cameraman flew into a rage saying it was dangerous and he was "walking off the set"

Out of Africa, into a chilly experience

My responsibility as producer was also turned to in a quite
major way when we were filming *Amundsen* in Norway. We
hired a local group whose hobby it was to re-enact period
exploration, who had the correct costumes and period sleds
pulled by huskies. We filmed them crossing a plateau which
looked eerily like the Antarctic. We had some of the best actors
that Norway had produced playing the parts of Amundsen and
his team. The filming required a replica of the interior of the
base camp hut they had built. We constructed this in the
community hall in Finse, a village round a railway junction.
When we tried to turn on the film lighting, it appeared that
we'd blown the fuses. However, somebody coming across from
the hotel reported that the whole village had been plunged into
darkness. The electricians and I assumed that this was some sort
of electrical sub-station failure. I adjourned the team to the
hotel for an early evening meal. This was difficult, because it
had to be cold food, but there was plentiful smoked salmon
and other Norwegian fare, lit by candles. In the middle of this
rather festive scene my electricians appeared, looking a lot less

cheerful than they usually were. In checking where the fault in the electricity supply lay, they had discovered that the village hall and indeed the whole village, was running on electricity that was being diverted from the supply for the railway. At this point a man in a suit came in. I recognised him as the mayor of the village, who had greeted us when we first arrived. He looked troubled. "You've caused more problems in the village than you can imagine," he said. "How is that?" I asked, feeling somewhat indignant. It became apparent that the town had illicitly been taking their power from the railway supply for many years. The mayor explained that, though it was custom and practice, there was no formal permission. "I'm sorry that we've caused the power outage," I said, "but how were we to know the history of your power supply?" The mayor said "I understand your position, but you'll have to come with me to meet the electricity company representative. He's on his way up on the next train." I agreed. The meeting was a bit like an attempt to bring peace to warring tribes, who talked the same language but had different objectives. I was in the position of the United Nations peace-keeping negotiator. In the end the magic letters 'BBC' were a great help and the mayor and the electricity company representatives agreed that they would reach some sort of 'understanding' that allowed our filming to go on, while they worked out a deal. I never learned how they managed to solve the problem, but the whole peace-making process may actually have been speeded up by what, to me, was another diplomatic embarrassment: the national skiing championships were on television that night and the real priority was determined by the need to get that key sporting event in Norwegian lives back on screen. So we were able to carry on filming.

The villagers had been using 'borrowed' electricity for years

When I got back to England I told the story to Robin Scott

and said he might get a letter from the Norwegian Ambassador. In fact we never heard anything ever again. There was, however, one other crisis. Stan, our chief electrician, had a heart attack the night after the electricity incident and we were fortunate that a rescue team was doing a rehearsal for an emergency in the area. They had contact with the helicopter that was going to fly their 'casualty' to hospital. It ended up by flying our very real casualty to Bergen hospital, which was an hour or so's flying time away. The good surgeons of Bergen saved Stan's life and when I went to see him there he was very cheerful. Some weeks later, back in England, I learned that his GP, to whom he'd reported this incident, had sent him to the local hospital to have a checkup to ensure that the Norwegians had done a good job. Unfortunately during this procedure, Stan had another heart attack and died. It seemed that the *Explorers* series was beset, attended and pursued by misfortune. This was partly mitigated by *Explorers: Amundsen* winning a BAFTA award in 1976, beating two of the other films from the series that had also been shortlisted.

CHAPTER THIRTEEN

The Che Guevara story

M y next film was to be *In Search of the Real Che Guevara*.
I've always thought that the point of documentaries
should be to tell people things they didn't know. This was a time
when every teenager had a copy of that iconic picture of Che,
who they saw as the face of rebellion, which was selling as

a poster all round the world. For
every teenager, there were one or
two worried parents thinking that
Che was simply a Communist
guerrilla. The reality was much
more complicated and interesting,
but not widely known at the time.

The film was a co-production with Canadian Television (CTV)
and Bavarian Television, so there was sufficient funding for a
reconnaissance. I flew to Mexico, knowing that the Danish
commune programme was safely completed and ready for its
transmission, which was scheduled during my absence. I was in
Mexico to meet the man who'd written what was at that time
the only biography of Che, who had died only four years earlier.
Daniel James was an Associated Press correspondent for Latin
America. I had read his book and, over two evenings in his
delightful house in Acapulco, we had valuable conversations
about Che and the attempt to set up a Communist regime in

Bolivia. Daniel told me that there were two copies of Che's diaries: one had gone to the Americans via the US-trained Bolivian Rangers and the other had been smuggled out to Cuba by one of Che's followers. There was therefore a race between the Cubans and the Americans to translate the diaries into English. Dan told me that the CIA had put him in a posh hotel in New York to translate the diaries as speedily as possible. He achieved this, winning the race for the CIA and getting their agreement to writing a book of his own experiences chasing Che. In the middle of a hot sweaty night in the Marriott Hotel on the beach in Acapulco, I was woken with the sudden realisation that if I bought the rights to Dan's book, somebody in Britain would be bound to get hold of the fact that the source for the material was a man who had been working for the CIA. If it became known, this would have been a disaster for the film, for me and for the BBC, because it would have fuelled suspicions that the film and the BBC would lack objectivity on the subject. I got a taxi up to Dan's house to have breakfast with him and he invited me to have a swim in his pool.

I heard myself saying "Sorry Dan, but you're off the picture"

I accepted, realising that I was going to have to break it to him that I couldn't possibly employ him. I dived in and came up in the centre of the pool, face to face with him, and actually heard myself saying "Sorry, Dan, but you're off the picture." He looked a bit surprised and, bobbing up and down in the pool, I explained. He accepted his dismissal with good grace, fully understanding that the BBC's reputation was at stake. Because I'd learned the story from reading his book, I was able to make him a courtesy payment for my interview with him.

The film reconnaissance continued in La Paz, where I checked in to the Hotel Crillon and found an enormous fax waiting for me. To my surprise and alarm, it said that I was being sued, with the BBC, under the Vagrancy Act of 1838. This Act had been created to curb the nudity that prostitutes in Victoria's time had displayed to attract customers, which had greatly offended the Queen when she caught sight of it on her way to the Theatre Royal Haymarket. I thought I must be suffering from altitude sickness (La Paz was about 3,650 metres above sea level). I eventually got through on the undersea telephone to the BBC in London, to be told that the action was being brought by the National Viewers' & Listeners' Association, run by a lady called Mary Whitehouse.

I was being sued, with the BBC, under the Vagrancy Act of 1838

Their concern was that passers-by could catch sight of nudity on television screens which, in those days, were left on in rental companies' shop window displays. I rang my boss Chris Brasher, who said he'd got the BBC lawyer and a judge in chambers set up. But what had caused this and why was I involved? It all went back to the Danish commune film, which had just been transmitted. While I had assured myself that the steam in the shower concealed the nudity, I had overlooked that, to get into this sequence, I'd asked the cameraman to get a shot of one of the men getting out of bed. As the man swung past the camera we'd captured rather too close a close-up. In the cutting room we'd edited this out, but as a result of an accident in marking up the film, a few frames of male genitalia had crept back into the transmission version. Fortunately the judge in chambers decided that the wording of the 1838 Act was not intended to cover electronic images in the 20th century. I heaved a sigh of relief and returned to chasing Che.

Che was born in Córdoba, in the middle of Argentina. He spent his teenage years in Buenos Aires and studied medicine there. Indeed, he played rugby for the San Isidro rugby team in the suburbs of the city. At the time I was filming, the generals, known as the Junta, had taken control of a country in which political stability was notable for its absence. I had two local guides to help me through the minefield of Buenos Aires politics. One was a local photographer, Roberto Bunge and the other a woman of Italian descent who worked at the American embassy, Maria Luisa Iervolino. Maria Luisa took me to a tango club, which I wanted to film as an illustration of Che's background. Tangos were not the smooth, swooping dances of the West but were, I discovered, love songs shouted or croaked by manual workers in their evenings, to make a bit of extra money. Several became very famous nationally and Maria Luisa had chosen a particular venue where one of the most well known was performing. As he sang of loves found in joy and lost in sadness, we heard machine gun fire outside. Maria Luisa held me in my seat by the elbow and hissed "We stay here." After the concert, which had not paused for a moment, we walked outside. There was nothing there except a pool of liquid running off the pavement into the gutter. Was it oil from a cracked sump or blood from a wounded human being? There was no way of finding out as Maria Luisa hurried me out of what had clearly been a confrontation between the paramilitary and the resistance.

As she walked me back to my hotel, in a fit of 'joie de vivre' I leaped over a barrier which stood in the way of our crossing a square. Behind me I heard a click and a gasp. I turned round and a policeman was holding a pistol to my side. Maria Luisa spoke quickly explaining, I guessed, that I was a stranger in the city and she was my guide. She showed the policeman her American Embassy ID card and we were released immediately. This demonstrated to me the power that the United States had over the military rulers of the country. Later, when we were filming in Córdoba, we got together a group of young people to question them about their hopes and aspirations for their country. Some were very open and honest, in what was a safe venue.

Behind me I heard a click and a gasp. I turned round and a policeman was holding a pistol to my side

Some years later I wondered with some dismay as to how many of those lovely young people had been in the category known as 'the disappeared'.

Che: myth or reality?

What the film told the wider audience for the first time was that, aged 24, Che and his friend Alberto decided, before completing studies at medical school, to take a motorcycle up the west coast of South America. They went through Peru, Ecuador, Colombia etc and, like young travellers of today, may well have visited Cuzco, the fabled capital of the old Inca Empire. Che said he had dreamed of visiting the ruins of Machu Picchu there since he was a boy and this was the site he and Alberto had most wanted to visit. They then continued their adventure onwards through the Amazon Basin and ever northwards, spending some time in a leper colony and on a raft on the Amazon river. Che found himself meeting for the first time the indigenous people of South America, who were poor and to a certain extent oppressed. The turning point was in Guatemala, where he lodged in a bed and breakfast and met a woman called Hilda Gadea, who he subsequently married. Hilda was a Marxist and Che told her how shocked he'd been encountering the oppressed natives of the wider South America, the like of which he had never seen in Argentina. He asked what he could do to help them, thinking perhaps of medical service in jungle villages in the Amazon Basin. She told him he should go and see two brothers in Mexico who she thought could use his help. Thus he met the Castros. They had led an invasion into Cuba of a small guerrilla group, seeking to overthrow a genuinely cruel and corrupt President Batista. They'd been defeated by Batista's troops and had no medical help to cope with the wounded, who they'd had to leave behind in Cuba, so the Castros saw Che as an answer to at least one of their problems. What they didn't know was that he was to turn out to be a natural military strategist. Together they invaded Cuba a second time and this time were successful, using Mao's tactics of picking up poor and angry local peasants as troops on their way down from the High Sierras. Batista's demoralised troops put up little resistance. Batista fled, the Castros took over and the rest, as it were, is history.

The Castros were left having to find something for Che to do in Cuba, but by this time he had become a rather heroic figure who was likely to become more popular than the Castros themselves. So they sent him around the world as a plenipotentiary to drum up support for the new Cuban regime. He also spent some time advising revolutionary groups in Angola and the Congo. But what he really wanted to do was to carry the revolution back to South America, so he made plans to build a revolution in Bolivia, which had a very unpopular president. One of his visits to garner support for Cuba had been to East Germany where he had an interpreter called Tamara Bunke. She was extremely attractive and they became lovers. Subsequently it seems likely that she

Bolivian Rangers re-enacting the capture of Che

was a spy for the East German Stasi. The Castro brothers had asked the East German government to keep an eye on Che, and Tamara was to be their eyes and ears. When Che went to Bolivia disguised as a Uruguayan businessman called Adolfo Mena González, Tamara joined him. She was to become known as 'Tania the Guerrilla'. His campaign in Bolivia was successful until Tamara left some incriminating papers in a jeep which she lodged in a garage in Ñancahuazú, along the river from where Che was operating. The jeep was found by the Bolivian Rangers. They were in the pay of the CIA, who were just as anxious as the East Germans, but for different reasons, that Che should not succeed in South America. Eventually he was surrounded and captured in the Quebrada del Yuro.

Moments after Che's death

To bring the film to life, I arranged for some local Bolivian Rangers to recreate, on camera, the capture of Che. They set to it with gusto and soon bullets were flying over our heads. Russ Heiss, the sound recordist, couldn't believe how realistic the blanks sounded. "That's because they're using live ammunition!" I shouted. The cameraman and I were extremely worried, but Russ was delighted.

Che's story was nearly at an end. By this time he had been locked up in a schoolhouse in Higuera. There is some dispute as to who actually killed him, but it appears to have been a

Richard Leiterman behind the camera

warrant officer in the Bolivian Rangers, Mario Terán. The man who captured Che claimed that, contrary to some accounts, the CIA had wanted to keep Che alive for interrogation, while the president of Bolivia was concerned that any trial might become a centre of rebellion in what was a very volatile nation at that time. Che's body was laid out for public display in the wash house at Valle Grande.

Valle Grande, despite its name, was a very small town and I stayed in a sort of bed and breakfast on the outskirts, near where Che's body had been displayed. Bed and breakfast indeed it was: one evening I was about to get into bed when I discovered that one of the hens, which wandered unfettered around the establishment, had laid an egg in my bed – ready for the following morning's breakfast!

While in Bolivia in search of more understanding of Che Guevara, my cameraman the Canadian Richard Leiterman and I went to meet the French poet and diplomat Jules Régis Debray, who had been an associate of Che. Our motives were thought to be suspicious by the Bolivians and we were arrested and briefly detained. After questioning we were allowed to go. Richard was subsequently able to get some shots for me of the schoolhouse in Higuera, as well as Che's beloved Inca site at Machu Picchu.

Finishing the story

When I returned to Britain after completing the actual filming for *Che Guevara* I did not have a writer, having had to put Daniel James to one side because of his CIA connections. In addition I didn't have any research material except that which I had taken down when going round South America filming. So the prime search was for a good writer for the commentary, who preferably had a severe self-discipline about factual work. It turned out

The French House, Soho, in the 1960s

that a really quite famous journalist from the Sunday Times, who had won the Pulitzer Prize for his reporting from Vietnam, had been given a year's sabbatical by the then editor, Harold Evans. This was Nicholas Tomalin. He had originally been going to use his sabbatical to write a history of the National Theatre, but the more he got into the project the more he felt a total lack of engagement with it. I telephoned him and said that I needed a writer of his quality at short notice and that his lack of television commentary writing experience was no barrier. I, and some of my friends, could give him guidance as to what to do and not do when writing commentary, but the priority was to bring a rigorous

Che took pictures throughout his campaign

journalistic approach to what was a very contentious subject. Nick and I met in that traditional location for such occasions, the French House pub in Soho. We immediately felt at ease with each other and even more importantly, he was fascinated by what I told him about the subject.

A few days later I took him back to the BBC and showed him all my research notes (this was before the days of the internet), and the sort of research sources to which he could turn – the BBC Library in those days was a helpful resource. Meanwhile I was in the cutting room putting together the Che material that Richard Leiterman had shot for me in the various locations where Che had been, together with newsreel material and still photographs from Che's own camera. The latter I had acquired thanks to the naivety of the CIA, who had handed the local chemist in Valle Grande all of Che's films that they had found when he was captured, with instructions that they should be processed quickly. The wily pharmacist, as he processed the film, had copied the negatives for sale after the CIA had departed, and for a relatively small sum I acquired all his

Filming a gaucho cattle round-up. Argentina was the home of 'machismo'

material. As I assembled the film I was able to explain to Nick the main rules of commentary writing, ie let the pictures tell the story where they can and add words only where they can't or where further explanation is needed. He was a quick learner and almost immediately understood, to the point where he developed his own style of writing for television. When the film was transmitted, on 16th November 1971, it received a lot of popular gratitude: for instance when I was lecturing at the Civil Service staff college at Henley, the head of the college thanked me for having explained Che's nature and objectives, which had allowed him to both put his adolescent children's views straight and to weave it into some of his introductions to staff college students. Although the film didn't win any prizes, that sort of success seemed to me more important. It had been my intention to tell the story of Che in a way that enlightened people who might never have come to understand what lay behind the famous iconic poster.

CHAPTER FOURTEEN

Harnessing a talent

Nicholas Tomalin had proved that he could write for television as well as newspapers. He was something of an eccentric, as were many journalists at the time, and to me had always been a bit of a hero. But he was indeed unconventional and when I was riding pillion on his Lambretta as we crossed London, he suddenly dived down a mews back street, leapt off the bike and, leaving me holding it up with the engine running, I watched him cross to the door of a mews, which he then kissed with great passion. When I asked him over a beer later what all that was about, he told me that a very beautiful woman, Sandy, with whom he had had an intense affair, had lived there. She was married to Wally Fawkes, otherwise known as 'Trog' the cartoonist, whose second line of interest was as a jazz clarinettist – in my youth I had heard him playing in the jazz club at 100 Oxford Street. Nick's even greater eccentricity was to nearly destroy our chances of making a documentary about the sinking of the passenger liner *Lusitania* at the start of the First World War: I went to his hotel room while on reconnaissance in the south of Ireland, to pick him up to go down to the bar. Lying on his bed was an air pistol. I went, as we used to say in those days, "spare". Did he not realise that he was jeopardising both our freedoms – to say nothing

RMS *Lusitania* goes down off Kinsale. A contemporary illustration

of our lives — by taking a gun, however small, into the Republic of Ireland at that time? He had the most marvellous ability to produce an innocent-looking face, which he proceeded to do and put his arm round me to say "But they won't find it, old boy!" Luckily for both of us, they didn't. Nick's mischievous

My old friend, Chris Ralling

nature gave him a good understanding of children, in particular teenagers. My son Mark benefited from this when rowing Tomalin's dinghy on the Regent's Park canal. Mark lost an oar and Nick got very wet recovering it, but he never uttered a word of reproach to Mark — indeed he seemed to identify with my son's adventurous nature.

Nick's talents were to lead me in exactly the direction I wanted to go. I had always wanted to dramatise a documentary in the manner of the great initiators of the form, Colin Morris and Gil Caulder, and the work of my friend Christopher Ralling. It was important to have rigorous factual discipline in making such documentaries. Preferably you would have accounts of a meeting, or even its minutes, as a basis for the dialogue between characters. Inevitably this raised questions of personification distorting the account of what had actually taken place. By the time I came to this documentary form, much had already been achieved by others. I had worked in harness with a drama producer in the BBC, Leonard Lewis, on a series that tried to separate fact from myth in the story of Jack the Ripper, so I was aware of the pitfalls.

This next project was *The Sinking of the Lusitania*. The RMS *Lusitania* plied regularly on the Cunard Line between New York and Liverpool. It was one of the largest of the transatlantic liners and carried up to 2,000 passengers. On 7th May

There had always been a suspicion about the speed of sinking of RMS *Lusitania* – and it appealed to us as a journalistic investigation

1915, during the First World War, it was sunk by a torpedo from a U-boat off the Old Head of Kinsale on the southern coast of Ireland. The ship sank incredibly quickly, before most of the lifeboats could be launched and 1,195 passengers died. There was always suspicion about that speed of sinking, which was less than 18 minutes, and speculation over whether the Germans were solely responsible, or whether it was a calculated strategy by which Winston Churchill, then First Lord of the Admiralty, ensured that America would enter the war on the side of the hard-pressed Allies. Was the ship solely a passenger vessel, or was it carrying munitions from America to help the British? This question had intrigued a number of people, including one of Nick Tomalin's contacts, John Chatterton, an American deep-sea diver who discovered that the metal plates of the hull had been blown outwards after the U-boat torpedo exploded, indicating the presence of munitions in the forward hold. From this circumstantial evidence Nick Tomalin and I came to believe that the British Admiralty had deliberately risked the *Lusitania* and the lives of hundreds of passengers, in the knowledge that it might be torpedoed, though it was not possible at the time we made the film to get any confirmation of this. It therefore appealed to Nick as a journalistic investigation, and to me as my first dramatised documentary, using the device of a courtroom setting. There had been a Board of Trade enquiry, but the minutes of that were brief and primarily concerned with the routing of the ship and the behaviour of the captain.

In the absence of an actual full enquiry into the sinking of the

With Nick Tomalin on reconnaisance round the Old Head of Kinsale, to check on the distance from the shore at which the *Lusitania* had gone down

ship I believed, and Nick concurred, that a dramatisation of an enquiry in which all parties were represented, was the way to go. We would put the relevant evidence in the mouths of actors portraying the main protagonists. We would also devise sequences outside the courtroom demonstrating the British naval approach to defending liners in British waters. Various expert witnesses, called by the main representatives, were all to be played by one actor. The casting was important to me because I knew that my lack of theatrical experience meant that I would not be able to direct the actors in the traditional way. After consulting colleagues in the BBC Drama department I was able to find ideal artists for all the parts, including Lee Montague as the universal witness. The *Lusitania's* captain was played by Peter Barkworth and the Admiralty spokesman by Geoffrey Palmer. Graham Suter played the Cunard representative, the U-boat commander representative was played by Jack May and the chairman of the enquiry was Sebastian Shaw. The argument about whether the U-boat captain had been briefed that there were explosives on board was never proven and at the time of the film's transmission, we still didn't know for certain whether anyone in the wartime British government had known of the risks that the passengers on the *Lusitania* faced. Apart from the issue of the hull having been blown outwards, the other circumstantial evidence was that the course chosen, round the south of Ireland where it was known that U-boats were on patrol, was a risk that had not been taken by other passenger ships; on their way to Liverpool they would more usually pass to the north of Ireland.

Soon after transmission I was forced, on the *Late Night Line-Up* discussion programme, to face the young Winston Churchill

Actors and crew prepare to shoot courtroom scenes in the Kinsale Assembly Rooms

(named after his grandfather), who believed that the great man's reputation had by implication been sullied. This was a bruising encounter and I regretted that I didn't at that time have more than circumstantial evidence. After *Late Night Line-Up* the researcher on our programme, Ian Sharp, later himself a film director, discovered in the public archive in Newcastle a document that had been signed by the Board of Trade. This showed that the insurance for the *Lusitania* had been under-written by the British government, which was highly unusual. It did not directly implicate Winston Churchill, who had been the First Lord of the Admiralty at the time, not the president of the Board of Trade, though he had held this post before the war.

Nick Tomalin had turned out to have a talent for the sort of forensic interplay that courtroom drama required and he came up with a remarkably powerful first draft script. Together we honed it into a credible courtroom format, including a chairman who would intervene where required. We were to shoot the film in Kinsale itself and I negotiated the use of the Assembly Rooms in the town hall.

The filming was to take place at about the time of what was to become known as Bloody Friday in Belfast. While we were filming exteriors of the 'courtroom' I saw a crowd of women and children carrying suitcases, struggling up a path on the hill behind the building. I asked one of the local people who was helping us what was going on. "These are refugees from Bloody Friday in Belfast and they're seeking shelter in the south," he said. "Why haven't they come the direct route and crossed in front of the courtroom?" I asked; and he replied "They didn't want to interrupt the filming." I told him to bring any further refugees on the direct route and we would pack up filming for the day. It was a terrible thing to realise that the economic benefits of having a film made in Kinsale were regarded as superior to the welfare of refugees from the north. That night the local Chamber of Commerce organised a party for the cast and crew. Nick and I had told the head of the Chamber of Commerce that there must be no speeches, for fear of inflaming an already sensitive situation. "That'll be all right," he said, "I'm giving the speech myself." At the beginning of the party he stood on a chair and proceeded to launch into just the sort of speech that we had instructed him never to make.

Nicholas Tomalin

It began "I believe that in Ireland we asked for heroes and God gave us martyrs." That underlined the difficulty of our situation. Somehow the following morning we were able to resume filming with no concern about our presence from either local people or from the Irish electricians, who were providing the lighting. At the end of filming we threw our own party and invited some of the key locals whose help had been invaluable.

Before I could work again with Nick Tomalin, a tragic event took place which made an emotional impact on me like few others in my lifetime. At the start of the Yom Kippur War in 1973, Nick had asked Harold Evans, the editor of *The Sunday Times*, if he could go to Israel to cover the conflict. He was, as always, seeking to get as close to the fighting as possible and was heading with the Israeli tanks towards the Golan Heights, which Israel was determined to take back from the Syrian Army. At that point in the dusty chaos of the advance, Nick and a German photographer, along with their Israeli Army PR man, found themselves in their car ahead of the Israeli tanks. The PR man required the car to stop and turn round, while the photographer wanted to take pictures of the advancing Israeli tanks. He got out with the PR man, leaving Nick to turn the car round to head back behind the front line. As Nick did so, a heat-seeking missile came out of the sky and blew the car to smithereens. Later, I discovered an ironic postscript: in another car amongst the Israeli cavalry, travelling with a group of journalists, was the former Group Captain Peter Townsend, who had been romantically involved with Princess Margaret. When he saw the battle commencing, Townsend told his driver to immediately switch off the engine to avoid being a target for any heat-seeking missile. Sadly, Nick Tomalin did not have Townsend's knowledge of modern electronic weaponry and Nick's car therefore became a target in the way that Townsend's had not.

I was in Zaire working on *Explorers* when I read of his death in an airmail edition of *The Times* in my hotel in Kinshasa. The impact on me was indescribable. This was a man I'd come to love as well as admire and he had gone, literally, in a flash. I have seldom cried as an adult, but this was one time when I was not ashamed to do so.

Aftermaths

Perhaps it is not surprising that Nick had a lasting impact on me. He above all had a way with words, both in conversation and in his writing. I was certainly not the first or the last to admire this but it struck me years later, when I left work and was looking for a chance to express myself creatively in retirement, and I chanced across a newly-formed literary festival called *Ways with Words*. It met during the summer holidays at Dartington Hall, the unconventional educational establishment in south Devon. I found the speakers at the festival in those early years were a marvellous stimulus when I came to write myself. I became a patron of the festival and it was a joy to find one of my fellow patrons was the novelist Mary Wesley, who lived locally in

Totnes. At that time I had read three of her nine books and her 'way with words' was something beyond the literary; it was brilliant writing, creating emotional and even physical impressions. I suppose the novel of hers that had the greatest impact on me was *The Camomile Lawn*. From 1994, when I retired, I would go to the festival each summer. On one of the first that I attended there was an opening party to celebrate the formation of the festival. Across the room in Dartington I saw a tall, statuesque figure, clad in a long purple dress. She had striking

Mary Wesley

features and wonderful silver hair. Above all she had an aura which compelled me to approach her. This was Mary Wesley and nobody at the party was talking to her. So I asked her how she used words to create the magical impression of a beautiful reality. We talked for a long time, I as the neophyte when it came to fiction writing and she with a life of immense experience, both emotional and practical. She led me through some of the ways of achieving an impression of reality by employing a style of atmospheric and graphic descriptions of events. That was her magic. I never did achieve that for myself, but my admiration of her use of words helped me in my own writing. Above all she was gracious and graceful and you got the impression that nothing that she allowed to happen around her would be boring or of no worth. I will always be grateful for that first meeting. We met once or twice again but that initial magic was matchless.

Another connection from my programme-making days brought benefits, this time to my family. During the making of the Che Guevara documentary, I had a good relationship with Don MacPherson, the Head of CTV. He proposed that we swap houses for a month. He and his family could see London and England, and I and mine could see the beauties of Canada – the Algonquin National Park lay within a few kilometres of Don's house. So we swapped. We lived in their modern house in Agincourt, a suburb of Toronto, and they lived in our Victorian house overlooking Wimbledon Common. Its position and view allowed Don to forgive me for the fact that, by Canadian standards, the heating belonged to the Middle Ages and there was no air conditioning. What's more, where Don had left us a full set of instruction manuals for all the equipment in his house, I had scrawled out in my appalling handwriting a sort of instruction book for living in ours. In fact, the MacPhersons had a good time going to all the things they'd wanted to see in London and driving down to the West Country to see a bit of England. As far as the Bonner family were concerned, the swap was a huge success. We borrowed camping gear from Don's neighbours, hired two kayaks in the National Park and took along a good supply of food, having been warned to string it up overnight out of the reach of bears. We managed very well for four days and nights, but on the penultimate day I failed to string up the food in a sufficiently bear-proof position. So we spent the last night and day living on what, when we were Boy Scouts and Girl Guides, were known as 'dampers' or 'twists': water and flour mixed to produce a dough which we would wrap round a stake and bake over the fire. The only other food we had

On the penultimate day I failed to string up the food in a sufficiently bear-proof position

that the bears had not consumed was a tin of treacle and a bottle of 'medicinal' brandy, so our last night's meal was dampers with treacle, washed down by a small glass of the brandy. The following morning, as we left for the starting-off point for the National Park, we were amazed to see that a family of frogs had lined up on a log, seemingly to say farewell. Our daughter Alison had developed a sort of relationship with these frogs. They swam alongside her when she bathed and clearly they were sad to see her go! After we'd got back to the National Park access point, we handed back the kayaks and loaded the camping materials into Don's little Fiat 127. We crammed ourselves in, with the children shouting "We must have food!" Restaurants or shops were not permitted in the National Park and, as we left, the children spotted on the horizon the big yellow 'M' of McDonald's, which at that time had barely got a foothold in Britain. So, cheered on by the kids, we drove into the first McDonald's they'd ever been to and tasted our first Big Macs. Frankly, the adults were so hungry by this time that we enjoyed the McDonald's as much as the kids. I think all the children had two or three. But it was a successful ending to a successful co-production.

Through yet another co-production contact, we had an equally memorable holiday. The CBS vice-president in charge of expanding their range of programmes invited me, with my wife and daughter, to have the use of his apartment in New York. Alison insisted that we take the helicopter ride round Manhattan, having been on a boat on the Circle Line around the island the previous day. This was some years after my helicopter crash in the Californian desert. I had been asked more than once whether I ever experienced any psychological after-effects, though in fact nothing like that had occurred. However, as we queued to get on the Bell Jet Ranger helicopter, I had to climb past the pilot. He had the same beret, mirror sunglasses and tan as Steve, my pilot in California. For a moment I did have a flashback, which translated itself into a momentary fear for my wife and daughter of the helicopter crashing into the Hudson River.

CHAPTER FIFTEEN

Television by the people, for the people

From time to time, when I was back at Kensington House, I had been sent as a deputy for my head of department to a meeting called the Programme Review Board, which took place on Wednesday mornings to discuss critically the previous week's programmes. I became known for taking a fairly radical view of the BBC's output. At the time there was a movement to open up British television to the voices of ordinary people, not just within interviews and documentaries produced by the BBC, but for them to actually produce programmes themselves. A colleague called Rowan Ayers carried out an experiment based on some filming with one of his presentation assistants, at the Guinness brewery in Acton, west London. The young director concerned believed that the best thing to do was to let the brewery workers discuss amongst themselves anything that they wanted to talk about, not just their own work conditions or politics, but matters of interest that were not normally dealt with on television. When edited to a reasonable length it was a very interesting programme and Rowan Ayers proposed to Robin Scott, Director of Television, that further programmes put together by viewers should be tried out in a small slot late at night on BBC2. Robin Scott agreed to a short series, entitled *Open Door*, which delivered some quite startling results, including aspects of married life, the business of living on too little money, etc.

Alasdair Milne

The programmes didn't get a huge audience because of the late time slot, but they did get some good appreciation in the audience research questioning. A second series would have been justified, but Rowan Ayers had decided he wanted to go off to Australia. The new Director of Programmes, Alasdair Milne, wasn't willing to risk anything other than what he regarded as a safe pair of hands to look after this form of output, which was helping the BBC to be more open. So after one of the Programme Review Boards he asked me to go and see him. He put it to me that, since I was so full of innovative and sometimes unwise ideas, I should take over the running of *Open Door*. I thought about it for some time, and felt I couldn't turn it down because it was in line with what I myself believed, ie that broadcasting was too important to be left to the broadcasters. My job title was changed to Editor, Community Programmes in July 1974 and my pay increased to a princely £6,807 p.a.

The unit was given the upper storeys of a house in Hammersmith Grove in Shepherd's Bush, which people could visit without feeling they had to go through the intimidating security of Television Centre, Lime Grove or Kensington House. A small group of people from the original unit under Rowan Ayers had developed an approach that made members of the public feel at home, making the sort of programmes they wanted to make and see on television. Some of these were fairly extreme and involved nudity, or vegan diets, or any other aspect of life which television didn't deal with at that time. The only problems arose in the area of politics. People on the far right felt that they never had a chance to be heard on television and people on the far left, the Workers Revolutionary Party and so on, felt the same. It was very difficult to explain that there were legal limits to the freedom we were offering, but we went as far as we could to meet their desires. My assistant editor, Mike Fentiman, had been part of the original experiment under Rowan Ayers and was hugely valuable. We did manage to fight off our critics within the BBC and achieve some good: while we never really were able to reach beyond the boundaries of conventional politics, we did push them a little.

Mike Fentiman was the best interpreter of what could be achieved by what was becoming known as 'access' or 'community' television. I was very grateful to him; he educated me as well. An example of our difficulties would be with a group from the Indian Workers' Association. They had decided that being left out of British broadcasting was a racial slur and they wanted to have the then Director General, Charles Curran, an Irishman, arrested. The BBC lawyer quickly organised a hearing before a judge in chambers. By this time I knew that Charles Curran was on his way to Twickenham to see the England v Ireland rugby match and would not appreciate being marched off under race relations laws. Fortunately the judge believed that there were legal reasons why the Indian Workers' proposal could not be accepted. Such hearings were frequently held in the judge's home and this particular judge had just come back from being 'on the circuit'. While he was away the builders had been in and there weren't enough chairs in his living room for everybody, so I stood up by the fireplace, resting on the mantelpiece. When to my relief the judge found in our favour, I took my hand off the mantelpiece and found it was covered not only in dust, but that there was a five pound note stuck to me. What do you do in such circumstances? Unbelievably, I peeled the note off, waved it at the judge and said "My Lord, I seem to have become attached to a five pound note intended for the builders."

He laughed and took his fiver back. There were many barriers in the way of the development of access broadcasting and some were legal, but I don't believe any other incident quite matched the judge and the builders' fiver.

"My Lord, I seem to have become attached to a five pound note intended for the builders"

In amongst the difficulties of *Open Door* there were other light moments. We helped a group on Cromarty with a programme about resisting the building of an aluminium smelting plant opposite the island, that was going to pollute both the air and the water in an area of great natural beauty. I found that the secretary of the group was also the Company Secretary of the local distillery at Tain, which made the much admired single malt whisky Glenmorangie. During the war the company secretary had served as a first officer in the Royal Naval Volunteer Reserve, on the ferries that had been commandeered by the Navy from the peacetime ferry company MacBrayne, running between the mainland and the various Scottish islands. He told me that one night, taking an admiral across to a rocket range on one of the islands, a fearsome storm had blown up. The old MacBrayne skipper who was still in charge of the ship was battling with the waves when the First Officer had spotted the admiral climbing up through the storm to the wheelhouse. "He burst in and I caught him just in time to stop him falling", he said. "He looked up at the captain and said 'Skipper — tell me — where are we?' The captain, still fighting with the wheel, pointed a pudgy finger at the chart. The admiral peered at it and said 'Those black marks, skipper, they're rocks! We're doomed!' The skipper said 'Aye, admiral, if you're a-thinking that they're rocks we are

"Those black marks, skipper, they're rocks! We're doomed!"

indeed puggered [sic]. But if you're a-thinking, as I am, that they're fly-shit, we're safe!'"

Much of *Open Door*'s portfolio had a political dimension. This was particularly true when I took the series to Ulster to get the various communities to make their own 'party political broadcasts'. Sinn Féin remained aggressive but diplomatic in this context. The Nationalists were aggressive without any gesture towards diplomacy. Between them was the newly formed Alliance Party, which campaigned, for instance, to end the educational division between Catholics going to Catholic schools and Protestants going to state schools. One woman from the Alliance Party said, on-air, that when she as a Catholic had sent her daughter to a state school, the bishop had threatened to "withdraw the sacrament of Confirmation from her". As she said this, I realised how far from understanding the situation in Ulster I was, and probably I was not alone as an Englishman in this respect.

Another activity of *Open Door* developed from an item that had been devised while I was the editor and was more successful than anything I had created myself. It was called *Video Diaries* and it allowed people, using newly available light-weight equipment, to keep a diary on videotape, recording details and arguments from their own viewpoint. This could be seen as father to what are nowadays known as 'blogs'.

Joining 'the hierarchy'

Running *Open Door* brought me for the first time into contact with what, as producers, we knew as 'the hierarchy'. I had to have direct access to the senior executives of the BBC because they needed early warning of how close to the wind some of the groups were sailing, and I needed somebody of greater responsibility in the BBC to know and advise me how far we could let the groups go.

For instance, a group called Troops Out made a programme that sought to ask the troops in Northern Ireland to desert! Fortunately, I was able to help them imply their aims rather than use the BBC to advocate mutiny and desertion.

As editor of Community Programmes I was now a legitimate member of the Programme Review Board and went every week, so my critical approach to programming had become firmly established in the mind of the Director of Television, Alasdair Milne. At the meeting there had been more than occasional comments that Science television programmes like *Horizon* were scientifically accurate but had no story-telling quality that might hold the general audience. Alasdair Milne sent for me and told me that this had become a problem and, though he'd talked to the existing head of Science & Features department about it, asked if I could come up with any ideas. I said most documentary-makers have to find a form in which to tell a story and there are certain basic rules. I quoted the old military instruction of "Tell 'em what you're going to tell 'em, then tell 'em, then tell 'em what you've told 'em!" Of course this was not the actual solution but I myself had found that, if I could put some intriguing indicators early in a film that there were going to be surprising facts emerging later on, this could keep people viewing while the story unfolded. It was then important to honour that pledge, but preferably you should keep the audience waiting for the next development of the story until almost the end of the film.

This dialogue with the Director of Television, coincided with the existing head of Science & Features wanting to leave, having discovered he was much happier making programmes than telling others to make them, and at the beginning of 1978 I was given his job. Some time after I'd taken over I bumped into him, when he was once again happily making his own films, and he asked me what I thought of the job. When I said I missed programme-making, he said "I always thought it was like choosing women for other men to go to bed with!" So I set about rationalising the situation and got one of the best scriptwriters I knew, Antony Jay, to come and give a tutorial to the *Horizon* producers and their researchers. He was brilliant and though initially his audience had thought it a bit of an insult that they would have to attend a tutorial on story-telling, latterly several of them came up to me and admitted they'd learned a lot. Within three or four months I began to notice that the scripts of *Horizon* and other science films were becoming more effective in holding their audience.

"I always thought it was like choosing women for other men to go to bed with!"

General Science

Besides the strength of my narrative sense I did actually know more than a little about the various sciences. I had wished to become a medical man – not necessarily a doctor, but I would have been happy to have been involved in pathology or, better still, the use of life-saving equipment. This had started when I was working in the PR department at E K Cole, the radio people, when technicians sought assistance in writing their instruction manuals in a way that was clear and helpful. My interest in such electronic and other apparatus also stemmed perhaps, in a slightly tangential way, from my building small radio sets in order to listen to comedy shows on the Light Programme under the bedclothes at school. I had started by building a crystal set, the circuitry of which was in a now defunct magazine called *Wireless World*. My father was friends with a neighbour who had been a radio maintenance man in the RAF during the war. He was a real enthusiast and had a complete electronic laboratory in his garden shed. I used to sit with him on winter evenings during the school holidays and he taught me a great deal. Eventually I graduated from crystal set to one valve set, to two valve radio and, ultimately, the king of such radios, a superheterodyne. That was my crowning glory. Unfortunately my version caused a whistling sound on neighbours' commercial radios, which interfered with their enjoyment. As well as electronics, I had a wider view of the sciences, derived from my attempts to get a First MB — an entry-level medical qualification. My maths wasn't good enough for the chemistry involved.

At that point I went into the Army and didn't pursue my technology any further, but it did give me some sense of the logic of applied sciences. My predecessor as BBC head of Science had hired a science journalist, Nigel Calder, whose father had been the science correspondent of the *Daily Herald* and who knew all the important scientists in Britain, including Nobel prize winners. Nigel and I did what was literally a flying tour of the top scientists of Britain to get both the contacts and some substance to my elementary science knowledge.

Healing a rift

As head of Science & Features, my major challenge was to get medical science back on BBC screens. The problem was not of my predecessor's making, or mine. The support of the medical profession had been withdrawn from the BBC as the result of a *Panorama* programme which had implied that, after some complex operations, the patient was pronounced dead while there was still a blood supply to the brain. I lobbied the British Medical Association to explain that the offending programme had come not from Science & Features but from Current Affairs. Not surprisingly they did not understand or accept this very BBC distinction. I had to win the profession back by talking to key

The support of the medical profession had been withdrawn from the BBC. I had to win it back

figures, the most important of whom was Professor Walter Bodmer, the man who ultimately started the mapping of the human genome. He was the chairman of the BBC's Science Advisory Group. Walter was sympathetic to our problem and he recommended that I went to see a surgeon, Robert Winston, at Hammersmith Hospital, who might welcome public access to the complexities of his microsurgery. Robert was extremely helpful and agreed that we could film a pilot programme in which he would commentate on the surgery that he was carrying out. The only rule was that he should be allowed to make recommendations on whether a particular operation was appropriate for transmission. I accepted this, although it was actually against BBC practice at the time. As a result we got a series of operations on the screen under the title *Your Life in Their Hands* – echoing a title that had been used in an outside broadcast series in the 1950s.

Robert was to be hugely helpful to me in a quite different dimension. Jeni, my wife, had been diagnosed with cervical cancer. Robert recommended that she and I go to see one of his colleagues, an oncologist. Importantly, she was a woman and sympathetic to my wife, even though she had to tell us the worst case scenario, which was that Jeni, who was only in her thirties, might have only four months to live. The consultant took me aside and told me about an experimental technique which had been described in the *New England Journal of Medicine* which involved a substance called cisplatin. I was in a bit of a state at the time and said to the consultant that she was doing what doctors in the Middle Ages had done which was, when in doubt, use a 'noble metal'. The consultant was outraged but gave me a photocopy of the *New England Journal* account. The experiment had been on a very small sample – not more than 70 cases – but the cancer had been defeated by more than the rate of chance. I went back to Jenifer and told her about this. I said that I couldn't decide for her and asked if she would consider becoming a trial patient. She felt there was nothing to lose and, courageous as ever, she agreed to go ahead. There had to be an operation to remove the cancerous uterus and what was removed had to be checked to see that all signs of the cancer had been eradicated. The consultant's registrar, a doctor called Elizabeth Whipp, was in charge of checking the pathology for any signs of cancer remaining. It was a long operation and I asked Liz to ring me when it was completed. I was sitting at home, in those days before mobile phones, waiting for the call. When it came, Liz said "It's a fucking miracle – and I don't use that word lightly." I said "Which word?" She said "Miracle!" Jenifer lived for another forty years.

"It's a fucking miracle – and I don't use that word lightly!"

After the success of *Your Life in Their Hands*, which was transmitted on BBC2, I was able to find a production team to work on a popular medical programme for BBC1 which we called *Medical Express*. The idea was that it would offer medical advice of a generic sort that patients might otherwise have had to get from their GP, and getting it from television in theory freed up GPs' time. It got a longer-than-usual initial run, not because of that, or indeed because of excellent presenters such as John Stapleton, but because Bill Cotton, who had become Controller of BBC1, had a tendency to hypochondria. When I put up the idea to him, he immediately said "How many can I have?", where for other programmes he would have asked "How much does it cost?" In fact it was a cheap, studio-based format that provided the sort of medical advice that was later purveyed in *Trust Me, I'm a Doctor*.

Popularising science

I also introduced a few non-science presenters for specific programmes. It so happened that it was the year of the centenary of Einstein's birth and, with some excellent producers, I persuaded Peter Ustinov to present a series on Einstein and his theory of relativity, for BBC2. I first met Ustinov when together we were exploring the possibility of making a film on the rail journey from Moscow to Vladivostok. He was fluent in Russian. That was one of my documentary 'fish that got away' – not the last time a promising idea had not been properly sold on my behalf to the channel controller.

Peter Ustinov

Another such example was a series about the iron curtain, which at that time divided the West from the communist East. There were varying degrees of fortification that ran from Finland, down through the strategically-important, divided Germany and the borders of Czechoslovakia, Austria and Hungary. This continued through the complex political and military situation in Greece, finally ending up in southern Turkey. I offered a series of 13 programmes with a commentary by James Cameron, the distinguished foreign affairs correspondent. It would have sold in its original form, but when the Berlin wall fell and Russia went through the period of glasnost in 1989, it would have made the BBC money from all around the world. This was one programme that certainly should have been snapped up by the programme controller.

Dudley Moore

While I was in Los Angeles dealing with the Einstein co-production with the local PBS (Public Broadcasting Service) station, I went to see Dudley Moore, who I was considering as the presenter for a more accessible telling of the Einstein story for BBC1. I was able to persuade him and Chris Hawes, a very bright young producer in the department, to make a more populist version. Dudley Moore was married at the time to the film star Tuesday Weld. When I finally found my way to their apartment in Venice Beach and Dudley opened his front door, he and his wife were clearly in the middle of a flaming row. My arrival seemed to act like a calming lotion and Tuesday Weld was too polite not to invite me to sit and chat, once Dudley had agreed to make the programme. It turned out that as well as being a musician and comedian, he was also interested in science. He and Chris Hawes got on very well and the programme was a popular success.

Dudley Moore and his wife were clearly in the middle of a flaming row

There were compensations for the self-denying ordinance of being a head of department rather than making programmes myself. One of those would appear to be a disadvantage: in order to get enough money to make such lavish productions, either additional funding or resources had to be found. This search for the extra cash was important in two ways. The official way was that it allowed the BBC to make programmes more lavish and, in the case of science, more attractive to the audience. As a head of department one had the benefit of flying to glamorous, or at least worth a visit, places like Dallas, where the local public broadcasting station had more money than it knew what to do with. I remember being taken by its president to the Petroleum Club in Dallas and sitting in the club restaurant, 22 storeys up. I looked around at the fellow diners and realised that the occupants of the room were certainly worth more than a trillion dollars between them.

Perhaps the most controversial co-production I did was with the San Francisco station KQED. There was a good-looking young scientist, Carl Sagan, who wanted to gain fame by a television series, and the programme controller of KQED was keen on the idea. It was agreed they would record Sagan doing the links in their studio and the BBC would provide the illustrative film. The series was called *Cosmos*. The Science department senior producers were a bit appalled by this adventure of mine and I would hear mutterings of "Caazmaz" in a Carl Sagan manner every time I walked down the corridor. However, to my relief, the series was a success – which it needed to be. The San Francisco station had also

Carl Sagan

provided money for specially written and recorded music to go with it and they produced an LP called *Cosmos*, which sold well – at least in the US.

But there were occasional dark moments: I was flying-in late to Colombia, the capital of South Carolina, to seek co-production money there. The flight was late, I arrived at the hotel at nine in the evening and asked for my room. The hotel had apparently lost the booking and when I insisted on staying, there was a look of consternation on the faces of the hall porter and the receptionist. "I think we have just one room left," she said. "I'll have to check." She finally looked up, turned to the hall porter and said "Room 385." I looked at the porter,

"Room 385," said the receptionist to the porter. His eyes widened

who was audibly controlling some sort of concern. He had the expressive face of a black comedian called Rochester in a television series that I'd watched. His eyes widened and appeared to revolve. I noted this, but by this time was desperate to get my head down and sleep; I had been travelling for about 15 days. I was given the key and told to take the lift to the third floor. I unlocked the room, which smelt strongly of disinfectant – but then many American hotel rooms did. I unpacked enough to get myself to bed and went to wash in the tiled bathroom.

There were flecks of dark red in the grouting between the tiles. I suddenly realised it was the remains of human flesh. It seems that sometime for someone in that bathroom, life's difficulties had appeared insuperable. Had I been less tired I might have given way to an impending feeling of doom. Instead I merely thought "Should I ask for another room? No, they told you this was the last one." I was so tired I just flopped on the bed and the next thing I knew there was light streaming through the window. I had to go back into the bathroom to take a shower. The horror movie sense of the previous evening had lifted and though I think the marks were still on the walls, I no longer noticed or cared. I went down to breakfast and by the time I got back up to the room, the cleaners had been in and the bathroom was literally spotless.

Next, I was able to go to Japan to talk to NHK, their state broadcaster, but they had a good science department of their own and didn't need major co-productions with the BBC. However there was a commercial station, owned and run by Fuji, the film and camera manufacturers. The BBC co-productions executive, who ironically was called Tom English, arranged for us to meet Fuji executives, and Fuji's president agreed to throw a dinner for us at the end of the working day. It took place at the top of Fuji's skyscraper. I had again been on the road for several weeks, visiting Australian and Chinese broadcasters, and as I got dressed to go to dinner I was horrified to discover I had a hole in one of my socks. In Japan you have to take off your shoes if you're in somebody else's building. Though I tried to cover up the hole as we approached the dinner table, the fact that the tables are practically set in the floor meant that, while I swung my feet under, for a brief moment the hole was visible. I was glad that nobody seemed to notice until Tom English said loudly

In Japan you have to take off your shoes. I was horrified to discover I had a hole in my sock

"Paul Bonner, you have just caused the greatest discourtesy to any host in Japan. You've got a hole in your stocking." I couldn't begin to explain to the president of Fuji that I'd been on the road by that time for more than six weeks. We did not get the co-production deal with Fuji. I blame the BBC rep's own goal.

The art of science broadcasting

Another Science programme issue was the fact that brilliant inventions shown on *Tomorrow's World* were somehow never turned into practical benefit to British industry, or indeed to public use. So I hit upon the idea of a prize for the best invention shown on *Tomorrow's World* that was actually taken into use and benefited the nation. I needed to find a person or organisation who would donate the prize. One of my producers recommended approaching the various engineering societies and associations for support. We chose the Institution of Mechanical Engineers, of which the Prince of Wales was an Honorary Fellow. The Secretary of this body volunteered to raise the matter at his annual meeting with Prince Charles. Charles was enthusiastic and a meeting was arranged in the summer for me to explain to him what would be involved in terms of a broadcast about the invention and the presentation of the prize. The day before my diary showed to be the meeting date, my secretary looked round the door with a worried expression on her face and said "It's the Prince's aide, Mr Cornish, on the phone." I picked up the phone and said "Good morning. I'm looking forward to meeting the Prince tomorrow." The voice barked back, with a harsh New Zealand accent, "It's not tomorrow, Mr Bonner, it's today!" A shiver ran down my spine. Yet again I was risking not only my career but the BBC's reputation. I said "What can we do?"

"I'm looking forward to meeting the Prince tomorrow." "It's not tomorrow, Mr Bonner, it's today!"

Mr Cornish answered that the best thing I could do would be to get to the Palace as soon as possible. "How will I get in?" I asked lamely. "I'll fix that. Drive to the North Gate." So I set off in my car, breaking all speed limits and praying that I might be stopped by the police, so I could say I was on my way to meet Prince Charles. When I arrived an enormous policeman at the North Gate looked down on me in my open-topped car. I said "You're not going to believe this, but I'm late for an appointment with Prince Charles." "I will believe it, sir," he said, "they've told me to direct you straight across the courtyard." I looked ahead and there was the Band of the Irish Guards counter-marching for a Changing of the Guard parade. I looked up at the policeman. "What do I do now?" I cried. "If I were you, sir, I'd drive between the mace and the front rank." I did this, nearly knocking down a drummer, and arrived at the north door. A gorilla-like man in royal livery seized me and threw me up to a colleague on the

"You must have had a terrible day. Would you like an orange squash?" asked Prince Charles

landing above. He threw me again up the final stairs, where Prince Charles was waiting. I arrived on my knees in front of him. He should have been irritated by this, my second transgression, but he was charming and said "You must have had a terrible day. Would you like an orange squash?" I said 'yes' and we sat down together. Who knows whether my strange arrival had amused him or not, but he agreed to present the prize to the winning inventor.

Another prize originated by my predecessor, Philip Daly, was for the *Young Scientist of the Year*. It was a Europe-wide competition, sponsored and organised by the Dutch firm Philips. The BBC's team reached the final, which would take place at Philips' headquarters at Eindhoven, but we all stayed in Amsterdam. The Philips' PR man, who handled the competition, invited me and the other English judge, Mary Archer, on a tour around the red-light district, a famous tourist attraction. Mary Archer was a distinguished scientist herself and was the wife of the author Jeffrey Archer. Mary, the other European judges and I walked, on a warm evening, along the canals that bordered the red-light district. In the illuminated windows of the apartments along the canals, naked women, many of them extremely beautiful, posed to display their wares. I watched Mary, who was a fellow Manager of the Royal Institution with me. She gazed at these figures and said "How can women so beautiful limit themselves in that way?"

The princes in the lab

One of the annual events in the life of the BBC's television science output was the annual *Christmas Lecture* for children from the Royal Institution. Though many controllers of television tried to get rid of it, the fact was it was very popular amongst families who had an interest in science, and indeed science teachers. It got demoted to BBC2 but it survived. During my final year as head of department the teenage royal princes, Andrew and Edward, came to the event, which was a lecture by an elderly professor showing the various forms of substances according to their atoms. The professor had set up a demonstration using bromine, which had a distinctive brown colour both as a liquid and a gas, and was therefore visible on television. It was also highly toxic. He manipulated glass equipment so that the audience could see the progression of bromine liquid into the gaseous form. In the middle of the demonstration he accidentally broke the glass tube through which the bromine was passing and it escaped, in its gaseous form, and started to drift across the lecture room towards the audience. To my horror I saw that it was approaching the royal princes. I screamed down the talkback to the floor manager's headphones "Get Bill to throw a blanket over it or something!" Bill, the lab assistant, was an ex-SAS man with an interest in science and he had the presence of mind — and the knowledge — to seize a bottle of ammonia and spray it over the brown cloud. It instantly turned into ammonium bromide, a white powder, which fell down on the floor just short of where the princes were sitting. I was mightily relieved that I had not been responsible for royal deaths!

CHAPTER SIXTEEN

Headhunted

Having reached the slightly-elevated echelons of the BBC, I had become chairman of the organising committee of the Edinburgh Television Festival, where serious matters of the future of television were discussed. I did not realise at the time that this would change my life in broadcasting in an extraordinary and rather wonderful way. I was to become the builder of the first new television channel to be set up, independent of the existing conventional broadcasters. The story is this: the key speech at the Edinburgh Festival is an event called the James MacTaggart Memorial Lecture. This was set up in honour of one of the best early drama directors. When I became elected as chairman of the festival in 1979 it fell to me to get the committee behind a single name to deliver the lecture. My view, and that of the majority of the committee, was that Jeremy Isaacs, the director of programmes at Thames Television, should give the lecture. He was the industry's favoured candidate to run the new channel. He had all the talents of creativity and leadership that were required. Some voices spoke against Isaacs doing the MacTaggart, but the majority were in favour and his lecture became known as "the MacTaggart application to run Channel Four".

The idea of Channel Four had a pre-history. There had been numerous proposals for the use of the spare frequency, which was known as 'the fourth channel'. The person who put forward the most thoughtful proposal was my old trainee partner in the days of *Gallery*, Anthony Smith. Smith spent five years as a Fellow of St Antony's College, Oxford. In 1979 he took on the notoriously difficult role of director of the British Film Institute. His success in that role meant that his views on how the fourth channel should be used were taken very seriously. There were various proposals from the Association of Broadcasting Staff,

Tony Smith proposed an organisation called the National Television Foundation

a union that represented primarily BBC staff, and various other voices from the media world, with titles such as Free Communications and the Association of Independent Producers. These came together in an organisation proposed by Anthony Smith, called the National Television Foundation. That proposal received considerable promotion in *The Guardian* newspaper in an article written by Tony Smith himself. The foundation encouraged the government to adopt various of the proposals and asked it to stand firm against ITV's fight to have it as their second channel, ITV2. The gist of these various proposals could be described as a channel with a neutral political stance, but offering programme airtime to a wide variety of opinions in programmes made by producers outside the BBC and ITV. Many producers had felt constrained by what they called "the silos" of BBC and ITV programme-making. Having experienced the making of programmes by groups outside the BBC in my *Open Door* days, I could see both benefits and problems with these proposals. In the end Jeremy Isaacs and I, and some experienced members of the group that was to become the board of Channel Four, devised a system of programme-making that would work, provided the money could be found. The political responsibility for broadcasting at that time lay with the department of the Home Office which had inherited the job from the old Postmaster General's department of the 1930s and 1940s. In effect, this gave the political power to decide on the form that Channel Four should take to the Home Secretary, William Whitelaw. At a Royal Television Society convention in Cambridge, he loosed a bombshell that would allow a new television channel to have finance: ITV would be allowed to advertise on the fourth channel, but would have to guarantee a certain amount of money ('the subscription') each year up front, to allow the channel to be set up and make programmes.

Soon after that there were interviews for the job of chief executive of Channel Four. Several senior executives, mostly from ITV, applied. I did not apply because I thought that Isaacs was the person best qualified to do the job. But one evening at home, I was rung by a member of the Independent Broadcasting Authority's (IBA) committee on the use of the fourth channel, to ask me why I hadn't applied. I said that it should be obvious that I thought Isaacs was the best man for the job and I certainly wouldn't apply. There was a pause at the other end of the phone and the voice said "We are not sure that Jeremy can do the job on his own. He needs your sort of support, somebody who understands the technicalities and priorities of getting a channel on the air." I said I would consider it, but in the back of my mind still not wanting to apply. In the end the chairman of the IBA's committee, Edmund Dell, himself rang me and asked me to go and see him. He reiterated more or less that his committee were not sure that Isaacs could do the job on his own. I was still not anxious to become involved. Apart from anything else there was a fair chance, if I stayed in the BBC, of promotion there. But I knew several other members on the IBA committee: Brian Tesler, the managing director of London Weekend Television; Bill Brown, managing director of Scottish

"We need your sort of support, someone who knows about getting a channel on air"

Television; and Roger Graef, an independent producer – and they took it in turns to ring me and try to persuade me. I was rather flattered by this attention so when, in the end, the IBA chairman rang me, I agreed to be interviewed. This was for a job that had, as many pointed out after the event, never been advertised and, indeed, had no job description. But the key meeting had to be with Jeremy Isaacs himself. Weirdly, before we actually met to discuss the matter we found ourselves filling our cars with petrol at the same garage in Acton. I asked him if the chairman of Channel Four had been talking to him. He glowered and said "Yes." We agreed that we would meet at an Indian restaurant in Hammersmith to discuss the matter properly. As the dinner proceeded I became more certain that Jeremy believed, as I did, that he could manage perfectly well on his own, selecting his own team of engineers, administrators and so on. But he was well aware that if he was to get on with

BBC Science & Features department's farewell to me when leaving for Channel Four

the IBA committee, which was to become the board of Channel Four, he might have to go along with their will. I also became persuaded that this was the sort of challenge that was more exciting than going up the ladder in the BBC so, when salary and pension were agreed, I tendered my resignation to the BBC, with my final date of work being 31st December 1980 – just over 25 years since I joined Programme Services in Bristol as a trainee studio assistant.

CHAPTER SEVENTEEN

A new sort of channel

I moved over to Channel Four at the turn of the year as one of the first three employees, in the role of Programme Controller. Jeremy was still finishing a series on the history of Ireland for the BBC and such administration as was required was still being organised by the IBA. In the event, the board were right, there was just too much work for one person and my strengths covered those areas in which Isaacs needed support. He and I, having known each other for some years, had an excellent working relationship, without which the channel would not have become so firmly established from its beginning. We had only until the start of November 1982 to set everything up and by this time we had to take on a building and have it refurbished, furnished and equipped for the administration and transmission of programmes; we had to appoint key staff, who were tasked with building their own departments from scratch, getting approval as they went, from Jeremy and me, for the more important aspects. I hired Pam Masters from the BBC as head of presentation. She in turn had to hire presentation editors and agree their staff.

One early controversy was over the off-screen announcers. We were clear that the voices would determine the character that the audience perceived the channel to have. The board were very keen on regional, non-middle class voices. The problem was, after three weeks on the air, viewers were complaining that they couldn't understand what was being said. Both Jeremy and I were determined that the first priority was clarity. I turned, as so often, to Pam Masters and said rather helplessly "What are we going to do?" Pam thought for a moment, paused and said "The answer is *English by Radio*." "What?" I said. She explained that in the BBC's Overseas Service in Bush House there was a small repertory company of actors who did all the voices for the BBC World Service's educational *English by Radio* programmes. They were renowned for their clarity of speech and Pam and I agreed to meet some of them, who had been recommended to her. In the end we kept the original announcer Paul Coia, a Scotsman, and hired Bill Bingham, Veronika Hyks and Olga Hubiczka from *English by Radio*. Veronika later took up a new challenge: the government had been successfully persuaded by the lobby of blind people's organisations who sought audio description on a separate sound track of the actions that were taking place on the screen during films and drama programmes. She and I were later to introduce her techniques at the European Broadcasting Union in Geneva.

The board were keen on regional, non-middle class voices – but viewers complained they couldn't understand them

The first automated channel in Britain

When Jeremy Isaacs and I found ourselves commanding Channel Four, responsibilities were divided as follows: ultimate responsibility lay with Jeremy. He also wanted commissioning editors – a term borrowed from the publishing world – who would choose and allocate money for the programmes that he sought to have. I set about gathering a team to actually build a channel. One of the senior engineering executives at Thames Television was Ellis Griffiths. A brilliant engineer, he had a certain rebellious nature that had required him to be seconded to the South African Broadcasting Corporation. There, freed from the tyranny of the broadcasting unions, he was able to devise an automated transmission system which could slot-in commercials and presentation announcements without the over-manning that had beset ITV for years. Whereas

The engineering team of Mike Sage and John Hazelwood, led by chief engineer, Ellis Griffiths (right)

ITV could afford the over-staffing, in Channel Four we certainly weren't going to be able to.

Our only income for the first two years of broadcasting was to be a 'subscription' from the ITV companies as a percentage of each of their profits. For that reason, ITV were anxious that we should achieve visibility in the market place. The ITV companies were very demanding in their approach to Channel Four being a credible advertising platform, and we therefore had to hire our own advertising agency. From a shortlist of five we chose Saatchi & Saatchi. Tim Bell, then their chairman and managing director, led his team into the interview with our chairman, Edmund Dell, Jeremy Isaacs and me, plus Justin Dukes, the managing director, charged with the financial aspects of the channel. Dell asked Tim Bell what image Saatchi & Saatchi had for Channel Four, from what had been written and spoken about it in the months running up to the launch. The response from Tim Bell was "We see BBC1 as a Rover 75, driven by an old man in an overcoat and a hat. BBC2 is a 2CV driven by a lecturer-type in tweed jacket and glasses, while ITV is a Ford Cortina driven by a guy in a leather jacket. We see Channel Four as another Cortina, driven by a Rasta, without the owner's permission." Asked what sort of audience they thought we

"We see BBC1 as a Rover 75, driven by an old man in an overcoat and a hat," said Tim Bell

would get, Saatchi's replied "Young and upmarket."

In the end the ITV companies negotiated a rather minimal amount, so the programme budget was very limited for the first two years. The IBA required them to guarantee the subscription in tranches that would keep us financially afloat, while not directly requiring us to sell our own commercials. Initially this did not make them the sort of money that they were paying out to us.

Setting up and setting out

The most important requirement from us was not to make our own programmes, but to commission them from independent producers. There were many producers of talent, both at the BBC and ITV, who were anxious to get away from the corporate ethos and commercial tyranny that they believed limited their creativity. They set up mini production companies in their own houses and were eager to present us with their ideas. The commissioning editors waded through a torrent of programme suggestions and thinned them down to the most likely possibilities.

The Channel Four launch team – including the first television commissioning editors ever – as featured in *The Sunday Times* **magazine, January 24th 1982**

Then it was for Jeremy, in the case of Drama — which he called "Fiction" — and me in the case of Factual and Comedy, to make selections, in consultation with the commissioning editors. For Drama, we were fortunate enough to get David Rose from the BBC, who was looking for a new challenge. For Factual programmes we had Liz Forgan, lately of *The Guardian*. There were one or two assistant editors in all the genres, handling specialisms like Youth programmes, Religious programmes and Music.

All of these commissioning editors in turn became almost overwhelmed with the applications for money and air time. We needed to get good

Visiting East Berlin, where state broadcaster Deutscher Fernsehfunk was a co-production prospect

programmes for the least possible money. We also needed to show our potential for the ITV companies to make money. We hired an excellent audience research expert who held a meeting with Jeremy and me each Monday, looking at the past week's audience figures. At certain points in the evening in our early weeks we received what became known as the 'zero audience' — in fact there would always be some people watching, even if it was only a set turned on in the corner of the room. But if there were fewer than 100,000, it registered on the audience charts as zero. Together Jeremy and I fought to get the sort of programmes that fulfilled our remit of making programmes that neither ITV or BBC were doing, while providing education, information and entertainment in the manner of the Reithian tradition of broadcasting. The commissioning editors reported to me and I chaired a rowdy meeting one morning a week discussing our successes and failures. It was quite unlike the BBC

Programme Review Board. The discussions at these meetings were brutal.

On the air

We went on air on Tuesday 2nd November 1982, launching with an educational game show, produced by Yorkshire Television, called *Countdown*. Before that there was a trailer, devised by our

TV Times **cover for the week of the launch of Channel Four**

Presentation staff, showing the range of programmes that we would be transmitting. It was this that was to cause initial consternation.

Ellis Griffiths and I hatched a plan to get people sitting on the edge of their seats by the time the very first pictures came up: we extended the gap between the test card and the fading up of the preview trailer, which traditionally would have been between five and ten seconds. This did indeed have the desired effect – in the case of Jeremy Isaacs, who fell out of his chair,

thinking that the whole system had broken down. But as he was rushing down the corridor to see what was happening, the music started and we were on the air. He threw his arms around me as we congratulated one another for somehow having got the channel on the air, on time and on budget.

Getting it right

Our concerns in the first half-year on the air centred on zero viewing figures, particularly and regrettably for the News. For this we'd allowed an hour, Jeremy Isaacs' view being that this would allow proper coverage of news stories in the way that the half hour of traditional news broadcasts would not. Unfortunately the editors, chosen by Liz Forgan but with Jeremy's agreement, were themselves not used to editing for conventional television news. Jeremy also was keen not to have, as he put it "shots of royalty or aeroplanes waiting at the end of runways." The news was using ITN's resources without their expertise because Liz Forgan and initially, Jeremy, wanted to get away from the predictability of 'packaged' news. The benefit of the extra time of an hour-long News was not immediately apparent to the audience. Eventually the board became concerned and a crisis meeting was held with our deputy chairman, the always-helpful Richard Attenborough. David Nicholas, who was the managing director of ITN, brought along one of his really top young editors, Stewart Purvis. Stewart impressed even the sceptical Liz Forgan with his combination of new ideas and the rigour required for broadcast news. After some discussion, we agreed to try Stewart as editor and he agreed to come to us. He was the third editor and the first really effective one. The viewing figures for *Channel 4 News* rose, never to fall again. It was particularly successful with politicians, who valued the knowledgeable approach that Stewart's presenters and reporters took. Stewart hired a former BBC presenter, Peter Sissons, bringing with him many years of skill in presenting and interviewing. Meanwhile, Stewart Purvis built up a team of reporters which met his high standards and this combination set *Channel 4 News* on the road to success. It remains today one of the most respected British news broadcasts. There have only been two editors since Stewart Purvis, both chosen with great care for their professionalism, and most of the reporters and presenters have stayed with *Channel 4 News* for long periods of time.

The benefit of the extra time of an hour-long News was not immediately apparent to viewers

An early *Film on Four,*
P'tang Yang Kipperbang
produced by David Puttnam

Fiction built a great reputation under the title *Film on Four*. The senior financial executive, who took the role of managing director, negotiated with the film exhibitors. He authorised his industrial relations manager to be very firm with the film unions, to ensure that Channel Four had a special agreement in relation to *Film on Four*. At the heart of its success was David Rose's choice of writers and directors.

An example of a risk well taken was *My Beautiful Launderette*, written by Hanif Kureishi and directed by Michael Apted. Some independent producers just wanted to make feature films and saw *Film on Four* as a huge opportunity. Working Title Films is an example, still producing today. The list of these bold but successful drama commissions was seemingly never-ending.

Another surprising success was in the area of comedy. Mike Bolland, who had worked with me in my *Open Door* days, was

Comic Strip Presents ...
Five Go Mad on Mescalin

a natural humorist of considerable intelligence. He went round the various comedy stores that were setting up in London in those days and found talent, which he put together in teams, most notably the *Comic Strip*.

Mike found an impresario in the form of Michael

White, who managed to hold the talent together, which no commissioning editor at Channel Four would ever have had time to do. Some comedy was produced by ITV companies on behalf of Channel Four, such as *Saturday Live* and *Friday Night Live*. Others were done by teams working together in the old Limehouse Studios in

Who Dares Wins

Canary Wharf. Out of the production unit there arose Hat Trick Productions, which is still producing good comedy today. With *Who Dares Wins* they had an almost instant success. In other areas of more minority interest like Religion, innovation was also forthcoming, taking a new approach to familiar subjects: for instance, programmes for a while were presented by a nun, rather than the usual type of TV presenter.

The biggest output of programming came from Education programmes. Naomi Sargant, who was the senior commissioning editor in that area, had a hugely valuable colleague in Carol Haslam who, as well as producing educational programmes, also commissioned documentary series under the educational banner.

The final important area of innovation was Sport. A group of us, led by board member Roger Graef, went down to the Odeon Leicester Square to see the satellite transmission of the Super Bowl final, which was paid for by American ex-patriots. Roger and I were very impressed by the response of the few British people in the audience. We discovered that coverage could be bought for British transmission relatively cheaply, so we tried it out. With the help of the Welsh entertainer Max Boyce, who we persuaded to be filmed training with the Dallas

Cowboys team, we launched a regular Sunday night event with American football. Another sport that benefited from Channel Four's existence was cycling, which had been more or less ignored by the BBC, except occasionally as an Olympic sport. Jeremy had the brilliant idea, when we were trying to fill the extra daytime transmission hours that we had been given, that we should see how much the French television networks would charge us for relaying the Tour de France. It turned out to be a very cheap way of filling lots of daytime hours. As Jeremy put it, "You can't lose with shots of the wonderful French countryside and a race at the same time!" These individual successes began to build into a successful whole and Channel Four was underway.

Revisiting the past

At that point I had a conversation with a friend, John McGrath,

Filming beside the Sweet Water Canal, more than 25 years after Army service there: Mark Littlewood, cameraman, with John McGrath checking a 'take' on headphones

the Scottish playwright who, with his wife Liz MacLennan, set up the 7:84 Theatre Company, touring with plays that he and others had written. This group performed in communities around Scotland and began to get good reviews for its productions, which were sharply critical of the social and economic unfairness of Britain at that time. John was fairly exhausted, as was I and, in comparing notes, we discovered that we had been in the British Army in the Suez Canal Zone at the same time. We'd both seen the impact of the stress that active service life had, in what was a mini-war zone, on 18- and 19-year-old boys. It so happened that I was in contact with the photographer who had worked with me in the PR unit in HQ British Troops Egypt and was now the staff photographer of *TV Times* magazine. With his memories in mind, John McGrath thought there was material if we could get those national servicemen to talk about their experiences, their fears and their joy at survival.

Jeremy Isaacs agreed that I could have three months' sabbatical to work with John on a film, which we called *Sweetwater Memories*, after the little canal that supplied fresh water up the length of the Suez Canal. He was the director, I was the producer, and our researcher was my friend Susan McConachy who John knew and who'd worked with me on *Choice* and *Bird's Eye View of Switzerland*. The young ex-national servicemen were not perhaps as coherent or interesting as we'd hoped, but their stories did illustrate the clash of adolescence with the harsh military world. During the course of preparing to film out in Egypt, we had to get permission from Egyptian, civil and military authorities who now ran the Canal Zone, having taken over after the British left. As a result of some of our meetings, we were invited to meet the man who had commanded the unit that had shot at me on the Tel-el-Kabir road thirty years before. John and I went to the apartment in Heliopolis to which the leader of Jamaliya Ismailia had retired. He saw himself as the victor, having helped to drive the British out of the Canal Zone. But he was charming, his daughters brought us coffee and sweetmeats from the female side of the apartment, and we talked long into the night. He didn't gloat over his success, but he left us in no doubt that he was proud of his role. Then came the most astonishing warning: "It will not happen in my lifetime. It will not happen in yours, and maybe

He warned: "It will not happen soon, but we Muslims will set up a caliphate that will dominate the world"

not in our children's, but we Muslims will set up a new caliphate that will dominate the world in the way that we once did." This warning was issued decades ago. John and I agreed when we left the flat that we would warn the Foreign Office as to what had been said. I rang when I got back to the UK and was passed on to a young duty officer, who said that he would see that the message was transmitted "up the line." In fact, of course, the rise of aggressive Muslim developments, Isil and the Taliban, is what we are facing today.

CHAPTER EIGHTEEN

Moving on

Jeremy and I stayed with Channel Four until 1987, when he went to become director of the Royal Opera House. Where should I go? I wanted to stay in television, preferably gaining new experience. One day, once it was known that I would be leaving, the phone rang and a voice said quietly "I'm about to offer you a job that it would be your first and possibly correct response to turn down." It was Brian Tesler, the managing director of London Weekend Television. He was a bit of a legend within

With Jeremy Isaacs at the Channel Four 30th birthday celebrations

ITV for clarity and fairness. His career had started as a BBC trainee and he had risen through the Entertainment side of British television. He explained that ITV was going to change from being a 15-part network to being more of a unitary organisation and, partly to anticipate government pressure, they needed somebody who was good at handling change. Since I had developed and managed a completely new television channel, the managing directors of ITV had thought that I might be the man for the task.

A voice said quietly "I'm about to offer you a job that it would be your first and possibly correct response to turn down"

The tradition of a parting cartoon continued when I left Channel Four for ITV. The cartoon references the series *Max Headroom*

Brian Tesler told me I would be well rewarded with better pay and pension for doing this difficult job. A start was made through the Independent Television Companies Association, which had existed for some years as a neutral meeting ground between the companies. It also liaised with the BBC in matters like the plans to televise Parliament. In the negotiations that followed, the broadcasters were all for it. The Commons was not supportive, but the House of Lords was – provided strict rules were adhered to.

It was at one of the meetings at BBC Broadcasting House about the co-ordination of educational programmes between the BBC and ITV, that I caught Legionnaires' disease, when the air conditioning system started to spray contaminated water droplets over the street below. The disease is very serious in that one's lungs fill up with fluid and you virtually drown. Luckily, my GP acted very quickly and

This was the ninth time I'd evaded the possibility of death

provided exactly the right type and measure of antibiotic that allowed me to survive. This was the ninth time I'd evaded the possibility of death. But I never walked into Broadcasting House again without looking up at the air-con units.

I returned to work and somehow we managed to corral the disparate parts of ITV into a fairly coherent whole and achieve the transition from a 15-company network to a manageable, more forceful single entity. With the help of Andrew Quinn, who had been managing director of Granada Television, I introduced a central programme controller, with commissioning editors in the special areas of Drama, Documentary and so on, as we had when setting up Channel Four.

Later, this experience was to be one of the factors that prompted the ITC and ITV to commission me to write two volumes of the history of independent television. This kept me active and in touch with the television business until I was 70, and ultimately led to my being awarded with an OBE for Services to Broadcasting.

Outside the Palace after the Investiture, with Jeni and sons Neil (left) and Mark

Because the companies valued their own sovereignty, the drive towards ITV cohesion was not an easy task. I became chairman of the Programme Controllers Group, where it was now apparent that a more coherent output of programmes could be achieved by central scheduling instead of programme controllers fighting for slots at the controllers' meetings. These meetings were what Brian Tesler had in mind when he had said that I might be right to turn down the role. It was like a bear pit, as macho controllers fought to get their programmes in prime slots. Their colleagues would find any weakness in the programme ideas in order to say that they shouldn't possibly appear at the time, or on the day, that was proposed. A lot of shouting went on until, slowly, one controller emerged as victor.

The meetings were like a bear pit, as macho controllers fought to get their programmes in prime slots

One aspect of the bear pit was the damage it could do to individual controllers and their companies' fortunes. It got so bad that a new Granada programme controller suffering from nervous anxiety was forced to retreat to the Gents, only to be followed by some of the noisier controllers, speaking loudly about his failings.

The controllers group was not quite out of control. There was a Network Programme Committee, which had oversight on the schedule to ensure fairness within the ITV network. Greg Dyke, in seeking to intervene on LWT's behalf at that meeting, sometimes ran out of words, leaving Brian Tesler to say "I sometimes think I'm only here to finish Greg's sentences for him."

The controllers group, in an effort to get difficult decisions made and, it was hoped, to bond together, were periodically allowed to go to an expensive hotel in the country to resolve their differences. At one of these occasions, at Eastwell Manor in Kent, David Glencross, programme director of the IBA and I were challenged to snooker by Greg Dyke and John Fairley of Yorkshire Television. David and I won, largely by dint of snookering their opportunities for sinking scoring balls. At the end of the game Greg said "It's just like you bleeding bureaucrats to get in the way of everything!" I gently explained that I too had been a programme maker and had made 28 documentaries in ten years, most of which had received a reasonable audience response. Greg went quiet and never tried to put me down again.

A significant breakthrough was when Granada, who had resolutely stood against their programmes being used at the weekend, agreed to a Friday edition of the great ITV institution, *Coronation Street*. But we still had to allow the companies to provide their distinctive and independent programming. An example was that the London Weekend company specialised in programmes that could stand up to the very strong Saturday and Sunday night scheduling of the BBC. The process of making a weekend schedule that could beat the BBC's took seven years. During that period we managed to wrestle the broadcast rights to the 1991 Rugby World Cup away from the BBC, which regarded rugby as exclusive to them. I was part of the team that succeeded in this and, by that move alone, we brought to ITV more upmarket viewers from right across the age range. This made the advertising sales people very happy. They, in particular, were already keen rugby viewers, as were many of the board members of companies like HTV, who had Gerald Davies, the famous Welsh wing three-quarter on their board, and Scottish Television, who were very supportive of our efforts. At last a battle against the BBC for rights to a major sport had been won outright.

CHAPTER NINETEEN

Farewell to broadcasting

I retired from active work in television in 1994. There were the usual (and delightful) leaving parties, but the most handsome farewell gift was flights and tickets for the Rugby World Cup in South Africa in 1995. Nelson Mandela was establishing the 'rainbow nation' and it was a fascinating time to be there. It was pure joy to be sitting in Ellis Park stadium for the final and see Mandela appear, symbolically wearing the Springbok rugby shirt.

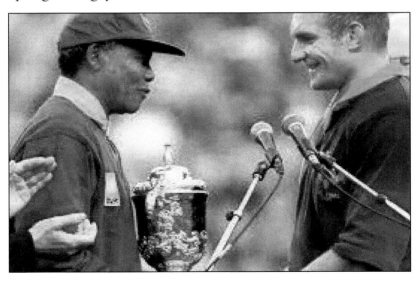

As a result of securing transmission right for the 1991 Rugby World Cup, I was given tickets to see the famous Ellis Park game in 1995

My retirement gave the opportunity to at last have my wife Jenifer by my side, travelling to places that neither of us had seen before. We had both always believed that it was worth seeing places in the world where there had been fighting or trauma, in their rare moments of peace and calm. In what looked to be a temporary time of peace between Jordan, Egypt and Israel we flew to Egypt and thence to my old army posting at Ismailia. We arranged to be driven across the Sinai Desert to the Egypt-Israel border at El Arish, where we stayed in the most flea-ridden establishment called The Moonlight Hotel, right on the Mediterranean shore. It was a romantic setting, which contrasted with the activities of the flea population. However, we had successfully crossed the Sinai. The next day we got through the two borders of Egypt and Israel and were driven on to Tel Aviv, where with much relief we had hot baths, clean clothes and good (kosher) food. We then followed the usual tourist route through Jerusalem and up to Bethlehem and saw the birthplace of Christ with its custodians from the Christian, Catholic and Eastern Orthodox churches. Finally we went up to Jericho. We flew back from Ben Gurion airport very happy, but of the firm belief that peace could not be maintained. Although there were still terrible tensions and occasional outbreaks of war between the Palestinians and the Israelis, in general the peace between Egypt and Israel is fragile, but has held.

So after this success, where next? Well, peace between the warring parties in Northern Ireland had been reached. Once again we thought it wouldn't last, went over there and took great delight in visiting wonderful spectacles like the Giant's Causeway, long before any tourists crowded upon them. The puritanical aspect of the Protestants evinced itself when we took

Jeni and I believed it was worth seeing places in the world where there had been fighting or trauma, in their rare moments of peace and calm

a bottle of wine into the bed & breakfast where we were booked to stay. It was seized from us, wrapped in brown paper and put away until we left. Other than that there were no remarkable incidents and a lot of beauty. I had been to Northern Ireland before for work, both when I was running *Open Door* and when I was with ITV, but I had never seen it with people happy to move about freely – though still wary when in certain areas that were not of their co-religionists.

Finally, we went to Odessa in the Ukraine, before it was retaken by the Russians, to see the battlefields of the Crimean War. To my dismay I discovered I'd had the picture in my head of the Charge of the Light Brigade totally the wrong way round. In my mind – possibly because of drawings I had seen in history books – I'd had the Light Brigade charging downhill on the Russian guns. In fact, of course, the reason that so many were killed was that they were riding uphill against secure Russian gun positions ahead. Fortunately in Sebastopol there was a wonderful panorama of the battle which told the story accurately. We ended our trip with a visit to Odessa and the steps where the most famous scenes of the revolution, as portrayed in the film *Battleship Potemkin*, took place. I was more fascinated, in this period of Gorbachev's Russia, to see the Russian Navy ships rusting away in Odessa harbour.

Looking back

These retirement travels were a bonus. I had retired on 30th November 1994, after 40 years in broadcasting. For me it was a bittersweet moment.

Many people have asked me what was the most exciting time in my life in broadcasting. There is no doubt that *In Search of the Real Che Guevara* was both exciting and satisfying. It was exciting following Che's footsteps around South America and it was satisfying because I was able to counter some of the myths about him; I was able to tell people who needed to know, what the man who'd become a false idol for the middle-class young was really like. Romantic perhaps, but certainly not the sort of hero that many had in their minds, nor was he as radical a Marxist as he was believed to be. He was, in short, an adventurer.

The picture of Che dead went round the world in a flash.

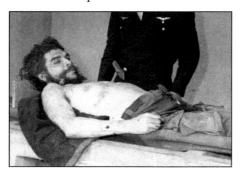

However, as well as proving him dead it had an even greater iconic significance than the images that teenagers put on their walls, because of its strange echoes of the classical paintings of the dead Christ. So, did I really counter the Che myth with truth? I hope so, but the worlds of imagery and storytelling are notoriously fickle because they are in the minds of the viewers.

I had spent, by that time, 25 years seeking to satisfy those fickle minds, while at the same time giving them some new insights into their worlds. It was a very satisfying job. The broadcast medium had given me a wonderful life and I hoped I had given it something in return. I didn't become the director general of the BBC – nor did I get the sack. I had been a medium man in a medium that I loved. One cannot ask for more in a life.

CHAPTER TWENTY

Travels with my Nikon

With my father's father a type designer and my mother's father an amateur photographer in the early 1900s – his darkroom was in the coal cellar – I suppose, looking back, that I was bound to be interested in the graphic arts generally. I couldn't afford my own camera until I was in the Army in

Egypt and bought a little folding Zeiss Ikonta for £6 in a shop in Port Said. It had no rangefinder or exposure meter, so I had to guess both distance and light. But in the conditions in Egypt, set to infinity and an aperture of f22, I always got a good picture. Alas, I was not allowed to take it when I went into the Nile Delta in 1954 for the El Alamein Memorial opening. It was not so much that the Egyptians had just taken delivery of

Russian bombers but rather that some Muslim sects believed that someone taking your picture was stealing your soul!

Back in England I bought a British version of the German Rolleiflex, which had twin-lens reflex focusing, and I picked up an old Weston light meter. I became an avid reader of *Amateur Photographer* magazine and entered tier competitions. I won a prize with *Two Eyes for the Night Train* (opposite). Most television and film cameramen working for the BBC were happy to talk photography – as long as you kept up an appearance of being an ignorant hobbyist!

Later I built my own darkroom in a pantry in our Wimbledon house, fell in love with 35mm Nikon cameras and took mine everywhere. I became interested in camera development and even joined the Nikon Historical Society.

There was no doubt that this enthusiasm did contribute to my career in television. But when working with professionals you must never let on how much you know about their craft. It has to be "I want the feeling of a Victorian steel engraving", not "I want you to use black and white stock and push-process it to 1200 ASA." I always remembered the radio producer Lance Sieveking saying to me, as the sound effects studio manager "could you make that door closing more like a brown leaf falling?" He didn't say "put a piece of cloth between the door and its frame and you will get the effect I want."

Respect the professional's knowledge, experience – and pride.

Two Eyes for the Night Train – **my first prize-winner**

Flying with a stunt team at Booker airfield

Portrait of my daughter Ali aged 11 through a 'grain screen' – a technique using the raw grain of an exposed frame. Was published in *Amateur Photographer*

Ducks on pond; and a mixture of spring and winter
Cannizaro Gardens, Wimbledon

A geyser in Rotorua, New Zealand. Catching it in mid-spurt was hit or miss

I enjoyed photographing the hundreds of orchids in Singapore Botanic Gardens

Spider's web by morning light

Rainbow over the Salute, Venice

The Rialto Bridge lit up for the Carnival

A gondolier

A domestic canal scene

I was experimenting with contre-jour photography

Rio de San Trovaso. Passing my favourite wine bar, Cantina del Vino già Schiavi

Postscript

Some readers will have come to this book hoping to discover how to get into television and, once there, how to get on in the medium.

No one person's experience is typical but in simple terms my answer is luck, having relevant talents and, above all, a determination to succeed.

One could add a willingness to work all hours until the job is done and to be a 'team player'. But, be warned, even those qualities carry no guarantee of success.

Bibliography

Che Guevara, A Biography
Daniel James. Pub: George Allen & Unwin. 1970

The Great Rebel, Che Guevara in Bolivia
Luis J. González and Gustavo A. Sánchez Salazar. Pub: Grove Press Inc. 1969

Che, Images of a Revolutionary
Edited by Fernando D. García and Óscar Sola. Pub: Pluto Press. 1997

The Motorcycle Diaries, A Journey Around South America
Che Guevara. Pub: Fourth Estate. 1996